S0-BJN-056

ENDORSEMENTS

Wanda Alger has emerged in a critical hour as a seasoned intercessor and prophetic voice to whom many must now give their attention. I could not put down the book you currently hold in your hands as I was captivated by her gift of writing and clear vision for the days ahead. Read the following pages with great expectancy and be prepared to receive fresh hope, zeal, and passion to see God's Kingdom manifested upon the earth like never before.

—Jeremiah Johnson
Best-selling Author
Founder, Heart of the Father Ministry and
Maranatha School of Ministry

What an *awesome* book this is! It is not just a book, but a true teaching tool in the hand of our God to help all of us fine-tune our role as intercessors, and to wield His Sword in *victory*. Thank you for writing this amazing volume!

—Sara Ballenger
Founder, Capitol Hill Prayer Partners
Washington, DC

Wanda's book is bold, balanced, and biblical! It is an absolutely fantastic resource to help us engage in effective intercession at this turbulent time in America's history. We are at a crossroads and dangerous precipice unless there is a spiritual awakening. Intercession and evangelism are at the heart of what's needed, so lay hold of this tremendous tool.

—Larry Tomczak
Best-selling Author and Cultural Commentator
Board Member, Intercessors for America

From Sword to Scepter resets readers' hearts and minds on heaven's perspective and purpose for the Church and government by arming prayer warriors for divine deliberation, declaration, and demonstration of Christ's reign and our response and responsibility to change the current culture through the power of the Holy Spirit. God has given Wanda a very powerful message, and I am excited to see how prayer warriors across our nation will take hold of this great guide to reshape our thinking and culture.

—Kathy Branzell
President, National Day of Prayer Task Force

Bravo! Bravo! Bravo! This is a handbook that will make history. This is an operating manual that I will immediately implement into many of the prayer meetings I lead. As an intercessor, recruiter, and mobilizer, Wanda's book awakens me as a watchman to my post. I jumped to my feet as I read it and cried out, "I accept the call as a watchman, O Lord!" My spirit was soaring as I said yes to the Lord, accepting this highest call of being a prayer warrior for the nation. The devotion Wanda calls us into of establishing prayer altars into every sphere of culture echoes strongly in my spirit for such a time as this.

—Bob Perry
Founder, Worship City Prayer
Team Leader, Pray Nashville and Nashville House of Prayer

Moving from
SWORD *to*
SCEPTER

Destiny Image Books by Wanda Alger

Prayer that Sparks National Revival:
An Essential Guide for Reclaiming America's Destiny

WANDA ALGER

Moving from
SWORD to
SCEPTER

RULING THROUGH PRAYER AS
THE EKKLESIA OF GOD

© Copyright 2020–Wanda Alger

All rights reserved. This book is protected by the copyright laws of the United States of America. This book may not be copied or reprinted for commercial gain or profit. The use of short quotations or occasional page copying for personal or group study is permitted and encouraged. Permission will be granted upon request. Unless otherwise identified, Scripture quotations are taken from The Holy Bible, English Standard Version® (ESV®), copyright © 2001 by Crossway, a publishing ministry of Good News Publishers. Used by permission. All rights reserved. Scripture quotations marked NIV are taken from the HOLY BIBLE, NEW INTERNATIONAL VERSION®, Copyright © 1973, 1978, 1984, 2011 International Bible Society. Used by permission of Zondervan. All rights reserved. Scripture quotations marked KJV are taken from the King James Version. Scripture quotations marked NKJV are taken from the New King James Version. Copyright © 1982 by Thomas Nelson, Inc. Used by permission. All rights reserved. All emphasis within Scripture quotations is the author's own. Please note that Destiny Image's publishing style capitalizes certain pronouns in Scripture that refer to the Father, Son, and Holy Spirit, and may differ from some publishers' styles. Take note that the name satan and related names are not capitalized. We choose not to acknowledge him, even to the point of violating grammatical rules.

DESTINY IMAGE® PUBLISHERS, INC.

P.O. Box 310, Shippensburg, PA 17257-0310

"Promoting Inspired Lives."

This book and all other Destiny Image and Destiny Image Fiction books are available at Christian bookstores and distributors worldwide.

Cover design by: Eileen Rockwell.

For more information on foreign distributors, call 717-532-3040.

Reach us on the Internet: www.destinyimage.com.

ISBN 13 TP: 978-0-7684-5179-5

ISBN 13 eBook: 978-0-7684-5180-1

ISBN 13 HC: 978-0-7684-5182-5

ISBN 13 LP: 978-0-7684-5181-8

For Worldwide Distribution, Printed in the U.S.A.

1 2 3 4 5 6 7 8 / 24 23 22 21 20

DEDICATION

I dedicate this book to all the amazing intercessors across this nation who have faithfully stood in the gap, stayed on the wall, and persevered through many challenges in order to answer heaven's call in praying for your communities, your churches, and this nation.

- I pray that the spirit of wisdom and revelation will come upon you as you read this material so that you will be encouraged, inspired, motivated, and enriched in your call.

- I pray that you will go deeper in the secret place to become even more intimate with the One who has called you and anointed you for this task.

- I pray that the strategies of heaven will be released in greater measure to see firsthand evidence of the Kingdom at work in your own sphere of influence.

- I pray that the anointing upon your life and call will draw others into the place of prayer, so that more prayer altars will be established across this land for the glory of God.

I also pray for the pastors, church leaders, and cultural influencers who will be reading this book.

- I pray your vision will grow and expand to see even greater possibility, destiny, and legacy that is awaiting us all.

- I pray for a greater love for the Body of Christ to capture your heart and empower your vision.

- I pray for the gift of discerning of spirits to be activated in greater measure so that you will gain confidence in heaven's agenda and boldness in confronting the darkness.

- I pray you will embrace your own assignment with greater zeal and increased passion for the coming harvest and the revealing of God's glory.

I also pray that the Holy Spirit would take the words I've written on these pages and go beyond the print to speak into your ears and write upon your hearts. May the message I share simply be a gateway for you to receive a firsthand revelation of God's purposes in this season. I pray that you will receive exactly what you need and that Jesus will be known, the Spirit will be revealed, and the King forever glorified.

Using the Sword

may destroy your enemies,

but using the Scepter

will secure your inheritance!

CONTENTS

FOREWORD

As one who has helped pioneer the whole concept of functioning more from a judicial perspective in the spirit realm than from a battlefield mindset, *Moving From Sword To Scepter* is a book that thrills me. What we are looking for in our spiritual activities is effectiveness, not just effort. The truth of the matter is that we have put in much effort and seen little fruit quite often. The Apostle Paul spoke of this in First Corinthians 9:26 when he uses a boxing concept to speak of effort being expended with no real results being seen.

> *Therefore I run thus: not with uncertainty. Thus I fight: not as one who beats the air* (NKJV).

Beating the air spoke of the way a boxer would train. They would shadowbox, which speaks of punching at an imaginary opponent. Through this effort they would learn to throw blows in a more perfected way, but they were not fighting something real or having any real effect. The result would be tremendous effort put forth but no advancement or victories being won.

So often I believe we have been beset by the same thing. Since the spiritual realm is an unseen realm it is easy to make mistakes and conjure up ideas that aren't real. We can invent imaginary adversaries we are fighting.

This causes us to use a lot of energy while thinking we are actually touching something in the unseen realm, when there is actually nothing there. The result will be no real breakthroughs. This in turn will eventually lead to hope deferred as a result of disappointment produced from having our hopes built up then dashed. Proverbs 13:12 uses this phrase to describe the condition in our hearts that can develop.

> *Hope deferred makes the heart sick, but when the desire comes, it is a tree of life* (NKJV).

We are told that when we have believed that something would occur and then it doesn't, a sick heart can be the result. This means that we have lost the ability and willingness to try again and believe. The root of this can be that we thought we were fighting an enemy that really didn't exist at all or at least didn't exist in the form we considered it did.

Another issue, however, is that the enemy does exist but we are approaching it from a wrong perspective or protocol. Most of us have been led to believe that we should deal with the devil and his forces on a battlefield. We are discovering however that unless we see the legal right of the devil revoked that he is claiming, we can never be effective in our spiritual warfare endeavors. Revelation 19:11 gives insight into how Jesus Himself deals with His enemies.

> *Now I saw heaven opened, and behold, a white horse. And He who sat on him was called Faithful and True, and in righteousness He judges and makes war* (NKJV).

Notice that Jesus in righteousness judges then makes war. This is the divine order. Judge speaks of judicial activity, while making war speaks of going to the battlefield. We can never win on the battlefield until we have first operated in the judicial system of heaven. This is where judgments come from. Through repentance we can see every legal right of the devil revoked and removed that he is claiming against us. In *Moving From*

Sword To Scepter Wanda Alger gives significant insight into the necessity of this. Key secrets to this effective way of function are also revealed. She helps us be able not just to beat the air in our efforts, but actually land blows on real opponents that will produce victories and breakthroughs. The result will be encouragement and healing of our hearts from any sickness of discouragement that has sought to possess them. We will again find not just effort but effectiveness in our spiritual activities. This will produce personal, family, business, ministry and even national results in agreement with the passion of God Himself. My prayer for you as you read *Moving From Sword To Scepter* is that the long-desired and sought-after breakthrough will become yours. You will see Jesus' longing over you fulfilled and over all that you love.

—Robert Henderson
Best-Selling Author of *The Courts of Heaven* Series

FOREWORD

I t's easy to be frustrated with the current state of our nation, the United States of America. It seems every "news alert" is about the latest negative event happening in politics that usually involves one politician criticizing another. Differences are emphasized, with each side absolutely convinced they are correct. It seems as if there is no solution and our only choice is to watch the nation, that has had the greatest impact for the Kingdom of God in history, implode.

And yet, what is God's perspective on the state of our nation? Is He calling the Church to act, or just sit back?

Wanda Alger's unique perspective on these questions comes from years of intercession, prophetic action, pastoring, writing, and leading God's people. Her practical answers to these questions will convince you what God's plan has been all along—how we are called to rule in the midst of our enemies and take action as believers.

I have been in ministry for more than thirty years, traveling the nation as a leader in different large national ministries; and I can tell you, Wanda's voice is needed in this day. Her clarity of revelation and ability to express it will encourage all who read this book. I currently lead a network of hundreds of thousands of intercessors who would respond to the type of teaching you find in this book. I believe that the Holy Spirit guides the Church to certain types of resources, and this is one of them.

Moving from Sword to Scepter guides you through the process of weeding out bad theology and replacing it with a practical mindset that will be aided by prayer points for you and those you will want to share with after reading this book. I encourage you to not only read it and take the time to pray through the prayer points, but to share them with others at your church, small group, Bible study, etc.

Moving from Sword to Scepter is a message for the Church for today. Do not delay in reading this book or passing it on. We are in a window of time that could quickly close; and unless the Church gains ground, we will lose our nation.

I have co-labored with Wanda for most of a decade and I can tell you that what you read in this book is personally applied. She's the real deal. Her journey has had many ups and many downs, many victories and some defeats, but she has remained faithful. The Body of Christ is now the benefactor of all of her effort.

Thank you, Wanda, for your faithfulness and tenacity.

—David Kubal
President and CEO, Intercessors for America

PART I

The GOVERNMENT
of GOD

Chapter 1

The CHURCH REVEALED

The Unexpected Trump Phenomenon

The election of Donald J. Trump to the United States presidency in 2016 was an historic event, not only for our nation, but for the Body of Christ. Never before was there such engagement in the electoral process on such a wide scale. Nor was there ever as much heated debate and division among believers concerning a national election.

In addition to the multitudes of voices yelling from the sidelines on social media, many unsuspecting citizens fell prey to the liberal media's bait selling a false narrative that dominated the news cycles even more than the actual facts. Many who found themselves lost in the sea of public opinion and media debate struggled to determine what was true and what was false.

Those who discerned the process from the unseen realm, however, saw something else. They saw a spiritual battle that was raging, far deadlier than the earthly one. The demonic forces at work behind the scenes were feeding a storm between the people of God and those who zealously opposed Him. Those who had been praying from the watchtowers of their homes and communities for years saw the anti-Christ agenda at work systematically and methodically undermining the very roots of our Judeo-Christian foundation.

These watchmen and intercessors became emboldened in their prayers and fearless in their determination to open people's eyes to the true battle at hand. Many prophetic voices had already been warning the Church of the spiritual strongholds at work in the high places of our nation in hopes of awakening those who had lapsed to the sidelines. If there was ever any doubt of spiritual warfare and the underlying demonic agenda lurking beneath the surface of our government, the 2016 election brought things to the surface as never before.

Both front-runners, Donald Trump and Hillary Clinton, presented huge problems for most conservative voters. Many suggested that the only alternative was to vote for "...the lesser of two evils." Yet, many prophetic intercessors sensed the battle was much more than just personal character or political agenda. If one were to judge only on the outward appearance by conservative standards, it would seem there was no "good" in electing Donald Trump. His personality and past record were anything but stellar, his lack of experience in political office was risky, and his visible lack of restraint and spontaneous outbursts were anything but statesmanlike. To many who were looking for godly character, not only was Donald Trump failing miserably, his reputation as a successful money-maker and savvy deal-breaker made him look like a power-driven, fortune-seeking egomaniac. To many believers, that just seemed... evil.

Hillary Clinton's platform and persona were just as unfavorable to many conservatives. Her progressive political agenda, including her support of abortion and championing of gay rights, violated core conservative values for many believers. To many, they perceived her political correctness as a façade. Her close ties to globalists and attacks on capitalism issued a clear warning to those who were feeling the sovereignty of our nation being threatened as never before. A vast majority of Christians felt her presidency would assure the downward spiral and erosion of our Christian heritage and conservative roots as a nation.

Even with these major deficiencies in both candidates, Trump still stood out to many who wanted change. Though he did not display the same polished presentation as the majority of his contenders, there seemed to be a molding and shaping taking place within Trump's heart. Not only did he invite conservative faith leaders to speak into his campaign, he began to openly speak of faith in God as a critical factor in our country's future. This bold declaration of God in the middle of an election cycle could have been political suicide. Yet, it ignited even greater hope among those who had been praying for a president who was willing to stand up for Christians. Trump's willingness to declare his commitment to conservative values fueled Christian voters, and many intercessors took it as a cue from heaven.

Divided in Discernment

One of the keys to effective intercession is having clear and accurate discernment. We are instructed to fix our eyes not on what is seen, but on what is unseen (see 2 Corinthians 4:18). Our charge is to look beyond temporal indicators and look from heaven's perspective in order to gain eternity's purpose. This takes a determination to not make hasty judgments based in the natural, but to look deeper into the spirit.

Even though many in the Church were stirred to prayer during the electoral process, it revealed a Church that was greatly divided in their discernment. It was most apparent when trying to figure out this man's character, motives, and fitness for office. Where some based their judgment on his outward behavior and personal history, others focused on his prophetic potential. Where many deemed him unholy and unfit, others saw a broken vessel that was primed and ready to be used by God.

For those who looked past Trump's spontaneous rants and impulsive tweets and searched deeper to his underlying motives, something else seemed to be moving him. Something else was driving him and giving him a bold and fearless demeanor. Here was a man who already had billions of dollars at his disposal. He already had power, prestige, and a fortune guaranteed to outlive him. Why would he leave his lavish life-style and continued success to seek an office with little pay, high stress, and guaranteed opposition? For those who looked beyond the outward appearance, they saw something else at work.

Though his early journey revealed the usual playboy activities and worldly pursuits of an unregenerate soul, it also revealed a thoughtful man who cared deeply for his family and his country. Even though his first two marriages ended in divorce, his marriage to Melania seemed to mark a turning point for Donald Trump. Not only did he make some life-changing decisions regarding his marriage and his faith, he never wavered on his commitment to his children. The fruit of his loins seemed to reveal something of the nature of his heart.

His grown children showed great admiration for their father. They were highly involved in his personal life and business ventures. And they all seemed to be healthy and stable individuals. Given the usual track record for highly driven business moguls whose children often pay a hefty price, Trump's children were different. They were truly a family, and they all seemed to adore their dad. This spoke volumes to those who were looking for a reason to support this man with the sordid past. It seemed his history as a successful father outweighed his history as an impulsive divorcee.

Not only was Trump's integrity as a businessman questioned, his motivation behind his leadership style was scrutinized. His party-seeking personality and love of the spotlight were labeled as narcissistic and self-centered. Yet, some considered how motivational gifts might be at work, seeing him as an exhorter by nature and prophetic in perspective (see Romans 12:6-8). This love for people was evident in his public rallies. It was face to face with his fans where he could motivate and inspire those who were discouraged or anxious. His optimism was contagious and stirred many to hope again. This same attitude was demonstrated even with his political rivals. Where other leaders put up walls and refused contact with the opposition, Trump flung open the door and welcomed them in. His bold interaction with potentially hostile leaders from other nations made him a force to be reckoned with, often silencing threats and accusations from those who would otherwise oppose him.

Many intercessors felt that the boldness Trump demonstrated was not just a personality trait, but a God-given zeal. His determination to face down his enemies and his persistence in accomplishing what he promised once in office, endeared him to many. Believing he was fulfilling a prophetic mandate, many saw this leader of the free world trumpeting a clear vision for the nation. Even in the midst of relentless criticism about his personal failings and questionable methods, this presidential candidate stood fast, winning him even more support from his die-hard fans.

Mercy Versus Truth

The outcome of the 2016 election brought some needed breakthroughs for conservative Christians, but it also brought some challenging barriers. On the positive side, the issue of faith in the public square finally became a worthy cause. Conservatives were increasingly unashamed in voicing their conviction about godly leadership in government and the need for faith to influence the public square. Prayer became a tangible force as believers across the Body of Christ began to engage in the political process. Seeing our core biblical values continually threatened, many evangelicals began to speak loud and clear demanding leaders with character, integrity, and accountability.

Unfortunately, this very value presented a major challenge with Donald Trump's leadership style. For those who wanted a leader with a clean record and pastoral approach to the presidency, Trump was one of the least likely candidates. Even after his election, many believers were challenged by his style, his methods, and his language. Regardless of the obvious economic advances of his administration or delivery of campaign promises, his leadership was anything but predictable or "presidential." The polarizing effect he had on many in the Church finally forced believers to deal with the underlying motives and priorities in their own hearts and minds.

In reality, what we face has more to do with who we are as a Church and less to do about a president. Ultimately, we are not in a war of political parties, but a war of principles and values. What we must rightly discern is the mission of the Church and the specific values we hold most dear. Until we recognize and deal with the growing gap of ideological differences and Kingdom perspectives, we will never come together as the Church toward a common goal. Until we come together on common ground, our prayers will be limited and our authority diminished.

Republican Christians need to face the reality that there are sincere Jesus followers who are still Democrats. As much as some would like to demonize the party, we must be willing to consider why it is that some believers hold fast. Reminding them of the platform and its support of abortion and gay rights has not been enough to bring us together. There must be engagement at a deeper level of conversation if we are to overcome our division and advance the Kingdom in the governmental realm.

I have observed that many who sympathize with the Democratic platform are focused on acts of compassion and social services. They value loving their neighbor, serving the poor, and aiding the disenfranchised. It is their heart of MERCY that pulls them toward those who have been victimized and it is this value that supersedes any other value or truth. Relationship is priority. For some Christians, they see the Democratic party as the champions of underdogs and saviors to the poor. Due to the party's inclusive language and cries for social justice, mercy-focused believers embrace this narrative, placing greater value on serving the poor than on necessarily saving the womb.

For those who stand by the Republican ticket, you will hear repeatedly their call for TRUTH. They are focused on what is right, looking for the facts, and holding to Constitutional law. They look for justice because they believe that truth is freedom. Even if it means a few relationships are negatively affected, they believe any temporary cost will be for the greater good. It's not that they lack mercy. It simply must yield to the truth in order to be meaningful.

Obviously, these are gross generalities, yet they represent some of the conflicting values among many in the Body of Christ. The heartstrings from one side are pulled by mercy and love for the victims, while others are calling for hard choices to be made for long-term benefit. Both principles of mercy and truth are biblical values, and thus one of the great divides within the Church. It is only when we as believers stand together for something greater that we will see the shift we so desperately need.

The 2012 Wake-Up Call

This need to stand together was here long before the 2016 election. Even in the 2012 election the Church was put to a test. The growing anti-Christ globalist agenda in the belly of the beast was already spreading, and yet many believers couldn't see it. There were those who believed the acting president represented a new message for a new era, and they weren't willing to let go of their dream for racial equality and social reform. In October 2012, a month before the election, I was given a dream that highlighted the realities we were facing and the dangers to come.

> *In this dream I was taken to the highest place of government. I saw the man in charge, and he exercised great power and influence. Though I couldn't see his features, the office he*

stood in was veiled by shadows and he moved as a dark figure throughout this administration.

I saw that things were not working as they had hoped. The tools of their trade in this place were breaking down and their workers were not being effective in their mission. I saw that these workers were actually pawns, unaware of the underlying agenda of their leaders and the true nature of their work.

Those in charge saw that the opposition was closing in on them. They began to collect weapons along with expensive gifts to be used as bartering tools. But where the workers were told this was due to an upgrade coming to the facility, another plan was at work. There was fear and panic.

As an observer, I knew I needed to act. This dark plan was going to hurt many people. I needed to try and intervene until help could come. I had my own weapon, but it didn't seem very powerful compared to theirs. Just as I was considering my next move, they realized their plans were exposed and did something drastic.

A type of nerve gas was released into the air. This gas affected everyone in sight and put them in a fog. This wasn't just a smoke screen. This gas carried the power to desensitize anyone under its influence. Not only did it blind them to reality, it actually caused them to laugh—to mock—to deny reality in favor of a fantasy.

I could see that the gas was coming toward me and I tried to hold my breath to avoid it. I knew I needed to get out of this place to keep my head clear. When I finally managed to get out, I went to look for my husband who is a pastor. When we got clear, we realized that all the police who had come were now inside this high office under this fog. They, too, were being taken under by this poison!

> *There wasn't any other help around. We knew we couldn't attract the attention of the enemy, but knew we needed to GET THE OTHERS OUT into the clear air. We knew that once we got enough of them free from the effects of this toxin, we could take the enemy out together.*

As I considered the spiritual ramifications of this dream, I saw a reality that could only be discerned in the unseen realm. I saw that the current president was under the influence of a spiritual force that was deadly. Those operating within the White House were being used and controlled by demonic forces, and many who were siding with them were totally unaware of the systematic national demolition occurring. Even those who believed their cause was just were being taken in by a controlling spirit. And now, the principalities at work in the high places of our government were squirming because of the rising resistance. It was the prayers of the saints.

The fog released in the dream was the enemy's counterattack to this increased intercession of the Church. Just like nerve gas is sent to constrict and immobilize its victims, the spiritual adversary released a spirit of deception across the land. This demonic toxin was causing thousands of uninformed and ill-advised citizens to follow a socialist pipe dream and laugh at anyone who suggested otherwise. Just as the police in the dream were taken in by this influence, so there were many authorities in the land who would end up crippled and powerless to intervene or stop the deception that was spreading.

> *Therefore God sends them a strong delusion, so that they may believe what is false, in order that all may be condemned who did not believe the truth but had pleasure in unrighteousness* (2 Thessalonians 2:11-12).

Not only does this describe the realities of chaos and confusion that permeate our culture, it highlights the desperate need for the Church to come together to fight a common enemy. Our battle is not against a man or a party, but a spiritual opponent who will stop at nothing to steal, kill, and destroy our national heritage and biblical foundation. In the dream, even the police couldn't stop the madness. The earthly authorities were taken out by the same deception, reminding us that our freedom must come from another, higher authority.

It is the watchmen and interceding believers who stay clear of the toxin and keep a clear mind that will be positioned to take action and break the spell. The Church, the Ekklesia of God, is heaven's change agent that has been called to go into those places of darkness and deception in order to set people free and see the House cleared of the poison. Rather than simply saving ourselves, our mandate is to bring truth and light where it's needed the most—the gates of hell.

The dream also revealed something else. It revealed how few of us there are.

Knowing the spiritual battle at hand in the 2012 election, thousands of intercessors were praying for a turnaround in the White House in the months preceding the election. Seeing the growing aggression toward people of faith and the increased hostility toward conservative Christian values, many were praying that a new president would be elected, and a new message promoted. Many prayers were focused for this breakthrough.

It was just a few days before this election when I was in a time of prayer, pressing into the need for breakthrough. All the sudden, Holy Spirit stopped me with these questions, "What does the Body of Christ need MOST in order to rise up and end this enemy occupation? What outcome would assure believers taking their place in the culture as powerful change agents?"

These were questions I had never stopped to consider before. I had simply always assumed God's plan was to change the leadership and political agenda, which so openly opposed Him and start over. I also assumed that we were ready. Certainly, it was God's plan to end this chapter and put things in order! However, these unexpected questions struck my spirit like a punch in the gut. Immediately, I knew the answer—and it wasn't what I expected or what I had been praying for.

I suddenly knew that there would be no changing of the guard. Any hope for a new leader or new agenda was being put on hold. The Church wasn't ready. In an instant, I was flooded with a terror of the painful realities to come. Personal values and religious mindsets were going to be tested and tried. The unrest and increased pressure on many in the Christian community would be felt as never before. And yet, I was also overwhelmed with an incredible hope, seeing God's ultimate purpose in mind—to prepare the Body of Christ, the rising Ekklesia.

At that point in time, the remnant who saw the brewing storm in the heavenlies was still relatively small and outnumbered. Those who were willing to step into this protracted engagement of political persuasion and governmental influence were few and far between. The harsh reality was that the Church wasn't equipped or prepared for what heaven wanted to grant us. We weren't unified nor did we even have a common goal. We were scattered and unorganized.

The Lord revealed that it was going to take another four years of anti-God leadership to wake up the sleeping Church and mobilize apathetic believers. Though it wasn't His first choice, He was allowing this chain of events to unfold in order to stir His Bride—the Church—to action.

We Need a Legacy

A lot can happen in a few years. Though we don't like to admit it, most of us are stirred to prayer and action when there's a crisis. The years between 2012-2016 were hard and painful, not only for the nation, but especially for the Church. The globalist agenda and demonic influence that a few had seen from a distance was now manifesting in city squares and community halls, and the grassroots movement began to rise up. Not only were Christians crying out for a change, but anyone who saw past the smoke screen of political correctness went to the streets demanding new leadership. The victory of Donald J. Trump to the presidency was like a breath of fresh air to many who were suffocating from the toxins of deceptive leadership.

However, as much as many rejoiced in the breakthrough of 2016 and a Cyrus anointing at work in the White House, the critical question remains: Can we occupy the land and steward our mandate long term, or are we still too weak, too divided, and too immature to take our place? How many national crises and divisive elections will it take to turn this nation around for good?

For those reading this in years to come, what will our descendants say about our watch? Have we prematurely celebrated entering our promised land of prophetic promises and Holy Spirit manifestations without addressing the squatting giants in the land? Do we have the courage to run into enemy territory to take down the demonic behemoths—or will we stay on the edge of our inheritance secretly hoping for heaven's cavalry to come rescue us from the battle?

We don't only need to turn our nation "back"; we need to disciple this nation toward maturity. We need to grow up. The cultural shifts needed and ungodly beliefs to be overturned are deep—and that's just in the Church! This will require not only persevering faith and targeted prayer, but practical application at every level of society for years to come. If we want to see long-term transformation, it will require a coming together of generations, ethnicities, genders, and values. It will require leaders with integrity and a vision for the future. It will require a prophetic perspective of the Kingdom in order to keep the territory we so desperately want to take.

It is the "Ekklesia" of God that has been formed and empowered to be the champions of this cause. This is the translation for the word "church" that is used 114 times in the New Testament. It means "an assembly of people convened at the public place of the council for the purpose of deliberating." It refers to believers who have been called out and set apart from the culture of the day, to sit at the city gates to rightly process and discern God's will and purposes. It is this Ekklesia of God that has been called to demonstrate Kingdom authority and blessing to the decaying man-made systems of the world.

This shift will require an upgrade in our intercession. The spiritual warfare practices of years past will not be adequate to assure the long-term establishment of Kingdom governance on the earth. Where believers have been consistently encouraged to take up the sword to fight their battles in prayer, heaven is now extending the scepter as a means of righteous rule through intercession. Where we have heralded spiritual warriors as champions of the faith, believers need to see themselves as rulers in heavenly places, executing justice from the throne of grace as kings and priests unto the Lord. This type of prayer is not merely changing our wording or methods of intercession, it requires a shift in our thinking and posture of heart. It will require a fresh perspective on our call to rule from a Kingdom position in order to legislate the affairs of heaven on the earth.

For those with the courage to face the challenge, it's time to put our prayers into action, become strategic in our warfare, and take our place as Kingdom leaders in this nation. As powerful as intercession is, without appropriate action and demonstration of that which we pray for, nothing will truly change. Until we have a clear mission of the Ekklesia and a viable vision for the future, we will continue to go around this mountain of indecision and division and never occupy until He comes.

PREPARING *the* WAY *for* OUR NATION

Of the greatness of his government and peace there will be no end... (Isaiah 9:7 NIV).

1. **Praise and exalt the Lord of the nations.**

    - *For God is the King of all the earth; sing praises with a psalm! God reigns over the nations; God sits on his holy throne* (Psalm 47:7-8).

        – Begin with thanksgiving (1 Thessalonians 5:18; Romans 1:8; Colossians 2:7).

        – Praise Him for His Kingdom at work in our nation (James 1:17; Revelation 11:17).

2. **Invite the Spirit of the Fear of the Lord.**

    - *Who is the man who fears the Lord? Him will he instruct in the way that he should choose. His soul shall abide in well-being, and his offspring shall inherit the land. The friendship of the Lord is for those who fear him, and he makes known to them his covenant* (Psalm 25:12-14).

        – Ask the Lord to reveal specific issues or situations where repentance is needed (Jeremiah 33:3; Proverbs 28:13; 2 Chronicles 30:9b; Matthew 3:8-10; James 4:8).

— Ask for the Fear of the Lord to come to bear on each
of the issues the Holy Spirit reveals (Isaiah 11:2, 33:6;
Psalm 31:19-20; 2 Chronicles 20:29).

3. **Bless all who are in authority.**

- *Where there is no guidance, a people falls, but in an abundance
of counselors there is safety* (Proverbs 11:14).

  — Specifically name and pray for elected officials to hunger
  and thirst for Christ and to seek His face continually
  (1 Chronicles 16:10-11; Psalm 2:10-11, 105:3-4;
  Matthew 6:33).

  — Pray for current leaders, both in the Church and in the
  nation, to be rightly aligned with the purposes of heaven
  (Proverbs 24:5-6; Psalm 37:27-28; Isaiah 1:16-17;
  1 Timothy 2:1-4).

4. **Declare a standard of righteousness.**

- *Righteousness exalts a nation, but sin is a reproach to any people* (Proverbs 14:34).

  — Pray for specific executive actions, court cases, and
  legislative initiatives to reflect the righteousness of God
  (Exodus 23:1-8; Micah 4:1-2; Deuteronomy 16:19-20;
  Isaiah 61:8).

  — Pray that citizens would rejoice in truth and pursue
  righteousness (Psalm 89:14-16, 97:1-5; Isaiah 26:9,
  32:1-6, 58:8).

5. Ask for spiritual revival marked by the Lord's presence and fruit of the Spirit.

- *Blessed are the people who know the festal shout, who walk, O Lord, in the light of your face, who exult in your name all the day and in your righteousness are exalted. For you are the glory of their strength; by your favor our horn is exalted* (Psalm 89:15-17).

  — Pray for refreshing and revival to come to the Church (Psalm 85:6-9, Joel 2:28-32, Acts 3:19-21).

  — Pray for an increased presence of the Lord to bring about transformation in our nation (Exodus 33:14; Hosea 6:1-3; Acts 2:42-47; Galatians 5:22-24; 1 Thessalonians 1:5).

6. Bless the increase of His government.

- *Your throne, O God, is forever and ever. The scepter of your kingdom is a scepter of uprightness* (Psalm 45:6).

  — Proclaim and rejoice in the supremacy of the Kingdom of God over the forces of darkness (Psalm 86:9-10, 110:1-2; Colossians 2:15; Revelation 12:10-11).

  — Commend to the Lord future generations, that they will be built on a sure foundation (Psalm 22:27-28, 145:3-13; 2 Timothy 3:14-16).

- *Blessed is the nation whose God is the Lord, the people whom he has chosen as his heritage!* (Psalm 33:12)

Chapter 2

RULING *in* THE MIDST *of* OUR ENEMIES

The Fear and Terror of the Lord

B efore we can look to the practical applications of Kingdom rule, we must get our priorities in order. We must see things from an eternal perspective and the heavenly blueprint for Kingdom authority so that proper alignment can come. Not only do we need a reality check on where we are currently, we must acknowledge the challenges ahead and find the path where God's grace and power flows that will take us to our destiny.

The enemies of God will continue to rise up to threaten and subvert the godly purposes and destiny of our nation. Those who are hostile to Kingdom values and righteous rule will increase in their efforts to sabotage any godly reforms in our government. The onslaught of villainous attacks against God-fearing leaders will continue unabated and it appears they will not stop. Any victory that is gained is quickly overshadowed by new accusations and threats.

As believers pray and contend for the president and those who serve in office, there is a command coming out of heaven. It is the same decree that King David prophesied in his own nation concerning the coming Messiah:

> *The Lord says to my Lord: "Sit at my right hand until I make your enemies your footstool. The Lord sends forth from Zion your mighty scepter.* **Rule in the midst of your enemies!"** (Psalm 110:1-2)

This is the righteous decree that must come forth in this hour and the posture of heart that must be taken by those who lead. Even as Christ demonstrated His Kingdom authority within a rebellious man-centered system, so we are called as emissaries of a higher order. We cannot wait for our enemies to leave or dissipate. We cannot hold back in hoping for some greater opportunity in the future. Our Lord has issued His decree and we must come into agreement. *It is while we are* **right in the middle of enemy territory** *that we are called to rule!*

Notice the keys in the admonition:

"Sit at my right hand...." It is only from this place that we have the eternal perspective needed to both pray accordingly and rule righteously (see Ephesians 2:6). It is from our intimate connection to the Father as sons and daughters that we can see things from His vantage point and share in His administration. If we are not seated with Him, we will be prone to react to things out of fear instead of deliberately establishing His Kingdom through prayerful response and appropriate action.

"...Until I make." It is not our job to make our enemies submit to us. It is God's. *"...He sat down at the right hand of God, waiting from that time until His enemies should be made a footstool for his feet"* (Hebrews 10:12-13). God is the One who deals with His adversaries, and it is our job to agree with Him in prayer by speaking His Word and declaring His purposes throughout the process.

"...Your footstool." He is not just making His enemies *His* footstool, but *ours* (see Psalm 8:6; 18:38). This phrase means that the enemies of God

must be subject to His rule. What He is establishing is a place of such Kingdom authority, grace, and power that no enemy will have the ability to overcome or overthrow it. Those who oppose His ways will have to submit because of the weight and influence of the King's presence.

To *rule* is not to lord over or dominate through force. It is a sovereign grace to administrate the purposes of God as representatives and ambassadors of His Kingdom. This is what we are to pray for our president and all those in positions of leadership and authority:

- To be seated with Christ, administrating from a Kingdom perspective (see Proverbs 21:15).

- To maintain a pure heart and clean hands so that the laws and decrees they make will represent the integrity and authority of heaven (see Psalm 24:3-6).

- To be strengthened with inner resolve and perseverance, even in the face of growing aggression and intimidation, so that Kingdom authority is fully established (see Psalm 125:2-3a).

- To be like Jesus who set His face as flint and did not waver on the promises of God (see Isaiah 50:7; Luke 9:51).

The Mountain of the Lord

If we are to see this kind of Kingdom authority established within the governmental sphere of our culture, there is another mountain that must be taken first. It is the Mountain of the House of the Lord that must be established as the highest of all other mountains. The Lord is calling His followers to come up to this mountain in the unseen realm in order to access heaven's counsel, wisdom, and might as Kingdom ambassadors.

> *It shall come to pass in the latter days that **the mountain of the house of the Lord shall be established as the highest of the mountains** and shall be lifted up above the hills; and all the nations shall flow to it. Many peoples will come and say, "Come, let us go up to the mountain of the Lord, to the temple of the God of Jacob. He will teach us his ways, so that we may walk in his paths." The law will go out from Zion, the word of the Lord from Jerusalem* (Isaiah 2:2-3).

Though the mountain of government is critical to the success of fulfilling our commission on the earth, we must learn how to rule from the spiritual mountain of the Lord from where true authority flows. Until the time when Jesus returns to rule in the flesh, He invites us to rule with Him on this mountain in heavenly places. It is from this place that God's Word and His ways *"go out"* to all the other mountains for Kingdom advancement. In this passage from Isaiah, the prophet also speaks of a day when the Lord's fierce presence will move from this mountain, securing His sovereign right to rule.

I had a dream in 2017 that illustrated this passage in a profound way. I knew the Lord was revealing heaven's purposes and how we as believers must prepare for the days ahead. Establishing *the mountain of the Lord will require sincere humility, covenant relationship, intimacy with the Lord, and a sensitivity to Holy Spirit's leadership.* The Fear of the Lord is about to be made manifest in a dramatic way, and the people of God must come together *as one* in *communion and worship* if we are to steward this call to rule.

> *I saw the Lion of Judah sitting on top of a fountain at the entrance to this mountain. However, He was very small and almost insignificant in size. He had been stripped of His*

mane *(the symbol of a lion's power and strength) and was looking into this fountain that was dry. There was no Living Water to draw from and He was focused on this desperate need. I could see that He was made from the same material as the mountain—solid rock—and yet was fully alive. He was obviously on duty, absorbed with the lack of water in this fountain.*

I then saw Man come and "shoo Him away" as if to say this Lion was in the way, not needed, almost like a child told to go and play. The gesture used was derogatory, as if to mock the Lion's very existence. I knew it was a picture of the Anti-God Man that did not comprehend eternity or heavenly things. He had stripped this Lion of His power and might and simply mocked the One who was sitting before the mountain. **Because Man was blinded by his unbelief, there was no fear of the Lord and no recognition of this One who was capable of utterly destroying Man with but one word.**

Yet, the Lion held back and did not counter.

The Lion ran into the mountain. Yet, I knew it was not running from something, but to something. I sensed it was on a mission. As I continued to watch, I then saw another Being emerge out of the mountain. He was fully alive, multidimensional, and not of this world. I knew this One was made from the very Rock that the mountain was made from. Just as the Lion was made from this Rock, so was this One. He came out and dove into the side of the mountain, creating another entrance. He was on His face with rock and dust falling all around as He created this new entryway into the mountain. I knew this One was coming directly from the throne of God and, in a posture of humility, was showing the way into this mountain.

> *Enter into the rock and hide in the dust from before the terror of the Lord, and from the splendor of His majesty. The haughty looks of man shall be brought low, and the lofty pride of men shall be humbled, and the Lord alone will be exalted in that day* (Isaiah 2:10-11).

I knew this was the Son of God who had made the way for us to enter into this holy place of the Father's presence and Kingdom authority. Humbling Himself unto death, He broke through the barrier through His own sacrifice.

> *Once this opening was complete, this One threw into the entrance four goblets along with a few other items. He was inviting us inside. As I walked in and saw the four goblets, I knew they were meant for communion. **We had been invited into this cave to share communion with one another and with this One of the mountain. The goblets were scattered to four corners and I knew it signaled a convergence.** It was a coming together from all four corners of the earth and we were supposed to take these goblets and come together. It was to be a time of sealing and agreement. The four winds, the four seasons, even the four rivers that originally flowed from Eden (see Genesis 2:10); they were all coming together with us to join in agreement for heaven's purposes.*
>
> *Even the goblets were made from the same material as the mountain. They were beautifully carved, but almost transparent instead of covered with jewels or gold. This, too, symbolized the need for transparency with one another, allowing the very substance of this mountain to flow within our veins.*
>
> *I was then given a hymnal. But it was not of the earth. It was from this place in the spirit, and the music within was not of*

this world. Even so, something within my heart recognized the music. We were all given copies of this hymnal and now instead of this One, there was Another from this mountain who was now leading. I knew it was Holy Spirit coming to lead us in worship.

As I started to sing from this heavenly book, my spirit began to stir and awaken to another reality. Man, who was beside me, struggled to follow along. Though there was a desire to understand this expression of the heart, the flesh was unable to access it. I knew it had to come from the spirit within in order to join in and receive its life-giving power. As we followed the lead of Holy Spirit, we were coming into this supernatural reality of the kingdom. Then, I awoke.

As I reflected on the many symbols illustrated within this night parable, the beginning of the dream caught my spirit as a signpost to the context of this deep message to the Church.

The fear of the Lord is a fountain of life, that one may turn away from the snares of death (Proverbs 14:27).

The Lion of Judah was watching over this fountain of life meant to represent the Fear of the Lord. But the fountain was dry. Not only was there no Fear of the Lord in the land, but the Lion Himself had been stripped of His identity and role. Carnal Man had stripped the Lion of His strength and power due to man's humanistic worldview. As I sought the Lord, my heart was broken as I felt His grief over the blindness of Man. The spirit of the age has stripped humans of their faith to believe in a supernatural God whose very power is love. I felt His passion—and yet His holiness which, when rightly understood, causes a holy fear that pierces the soul.

The Mountain of the Lord is a place where Holy Spirit leads and we follow. It is a place where differences are put aside and believers come together to gaze on the Only One worth our time and attention. It is a place of agreement and joy. It is a place hidden from the intrigues of man and the distractions of the enemy. It is a place without fear or doubt. It is where we come together to receive the grace that is needed, the power that is possible, and the perspective that is necessary, in order to rightly come into our inheritance as sons and daughters.

This dream also highlighted the necessity of the Fear of the Lord as being central to any needed shift in Kingdom rule. Humankind has yet to see and experience the *terror of the Lord,* which is also the splendor of His majesty. What the enemy is doing right now upon the earth is counterfeiting this Fear of the Lord with demonic terror. Where the Fear of the Lord keeps us safe and empowers us to live and move and have our being, the enemy's terror does the opposite. This can only be overcome by embracing the true Fear of the Lord in order to immunize ourselves against the counterfeit.

> *And the haughtiness of man shall be humbled, and the lofty pride of men shall be brought low, and the Lord alone will be exalted in that day. And the idols shall utterly pass away. And people shall enter the caves of the rocks and the holes of the ground, from before the **terror of the Lord**, and from the splendor of his majesty, when he rises to terrify the earth* (Isaiah 2:17-19)

The Fear and Terror of the Lord

The only two "open visions" that I've ever had have been within dreams—seeing something as if played on a TV screen. I had the first one in 2015. Though the dream itself had weight to it, the open vision within the dream seemed to punctuate the seriousness of the message. It was a picture of what was to come regarding the fear and glory of the Lord.

I was walking down a road with many people. All of a sudden behind my right shoulder, a huge golden beam of light from the heavens shone down and began to move across the sky in front of me from right to left. It was massive, and it was evident it was not man-made but from another realm. It began to engulf everything it touched.

At the same time, I looked up to my right and in the skies was a huge screen that opened up in front of me. On it I saw a map of the world. It was as if I was seeing and experiencing this phenomenon from two different dimensions—the natural and the spiritual. I saw this all-encompassing golden light start at the eastern part of the map near Australia and it began to slowly move west across the entire globe. The light filled the sky and was full of glory and power. It seemed to move across the center of the map, touching different countries at varying degrees. I knew that what I was seeing and experiencing was global and affecting everyone everywhere.

I heard myself shouting, "It's happening! It's happening!" and my heart began to race with excitement. This light was multidimensional. It not only went across the surface of the earth but went underneath in varying degrees of color and richness. The deeper it penetrated, the deeper its color and impact. It was powerful, distinct, and moved with ultimate authority.

I was immediately overwhelmed with joy and awe and fell to my knees as I realized the immensity of what was happening. I cried out in worship and adoration. I knew it was the weight of His glory covering the earth. Yet, even as I was filled with wonder and awe, I could sense the fear around me, the uncertainty of what was taking place. Though half of the people were caught up in praise and exaltation, the other half were on their knees in absolute terror.

As people looked up, dazed and in shock of what was taking place, I shouted out without hesitation, "It's coming! Heaven is coming!" I could see that for those who were not ready, it was bringing dread and fear. But, for those who believed... it would be filled with awe and thanksgiving. I realized then that the Fear of the Lord was coming in great glory and power and everything in its path was going to be affected. Depending on the state of each one's heart, this move would bring either worship and praise, or fear and dread.

There they are in great terror, for God is with the generation of the righteous (Psalm 14:5).

This dream and others like it have etched in my spirit the full expectation of a coming move of His Spirit that will change everything as we have known it. It will be a wake-up call, demonstrating the reality of *His* Kingdom authority and power. It will not be like any other past moves of the Holy Spirit. It will not limit itself to a few hungry souls but will permeate and saturate all in its path. The Lord Jesus is set on revealing the full weight of His Father's love, power, and holiness in order to energize and empower His Bride for the work ahead.

This move will destroy all double-mindedness, self-righteousness, greed, pride, and self-promotion. This move will cleanse us, refine us, purify us, and deliver us from the evil one's deception and trickery. It will expose those who are right with God and those who are not. It will shine the light in the darkness and all the rats and rodents of wickedness in high places will be scrambling for protection, only to find they have been utterly unseated and undone.

...they were all seized with fear, and the name of the Lord Jesus was held in high honor. Many of those who believed now came and openly confessed what they had done (Acts 19:17-18 NIV).

When we have experienced the true Fear of the Lord in this manner of power, the rules will change. It will no longer be the kingdoms of this world that will determine the course of history, but the Kingdom of our Lord and Savior, Jesus Christ! His ultimate authority as King of the earth will be made manifest, and those who serve Him out of a pure heart will be given even greater access, favor, and heavenly authority to rule in the midst of His enemies (see Psalm 110:1-2)! That which was by faith will now be made visible, and heaven's justice will be executed on the earth as He makes our enemies His footstool.

But it will not come without cost.

Things that are taking place, even now, should serve as a reminder that no one is exempt from trial, hardship, or pain. Being a follower of Christ does not guarantee an easy road or carefree journey (see Matthew 5:44-45). Those who are selling that kind of walk are peddlers and fools. The only "safe" place on this side of heaven is to be under the shelter of the Most High God and hidden in Him (see Psalm 91; Psalm 24:3-6). The access to that place is through righteousness and a holy life. There are no shortcuts. It is only as we rightly fear the Lord that we are kept from the enemy's hold and assured of a righteous reward.

We must be prepared. When this move comes—will we be on our faces in worship, or brought to our knees in terror? Will we rejoice at the tangible presence of His power and glory or will we tremble in fear due to the sin and compromise in our lives? Now is the time to turn away from excuses and apathy. Now is the time to embrace the cross and lay down any sense of entitlement to our lives. The Father is calling for absolute obedience, surrender, and holiness. There are no grey areas in His presence. He is about to burn up all His enemies and utterly consume the lies, the strongholds, and the idolatry that is poisoning the Church.

As we continue to pray for this nation and for our families and communities, we must pursue this place of communion and worship with one another. We must seek to establish the House of the Lord as the highest of all other mountains. We must learn to follow the lead of Holy Spirit as He teaches us the worship of heaven. We must ask for, and walk in, a holy reverence and awe for the Mighty One of Israel.

> *And many peoples shall come, and say: "Come, let us go up to the mountain of the Lord, to the house of the God of Jacob, that he may teach us his ways and that we may walk in his paths." For out of Zion shall go forth the law, and the word of the Lord from Jerusalem. He shall judge between the nations, and shall decide disputes for many peoples; and they shall beat their swords into plowshares, and their spears into pruning hooks; nation shall not lift up sword against nation, neither shall they learn war anymore. O house of Jacob, come, let us walk in the light of the Lord* (Isaiah 2:3-5).

A Charge for Those Establishing This Mountain

The psalmist prophesied that the Lord would send forth His scepter from Zion. The administration of heaven is issuing this decree to those being mantled with authority to lead:

Rule in the midst of your enemies!

This charge not only requires personal sanctification and absolute obedience, but a deliberate activation and mobilization of the Ekklesia of God. Before we can influence our culture and bear weight in the governmental affairs on the earth, we must first govern ourselves and our houses. It starts with the House of the Lord.

This alignment of God's governing authorities is signaling an increased kingdom authority to rule and reign, even as the enemies of Zion vehemently oppose it. We must agree with heaven and declare this in our prayers and our praises (see Psalm 2:1-6). As believers in Christ and ambassadors of His kingdom, we agree together for all those who have been called to leadership in this hour.

PRAYER GUIDE

THE FEAR
of the LORD

Declarations Over Our Leaders

The characteristics of the awe and reverence for the Lord are found throughout Scripture. Pray that both citizens and leaders would pursue, embrace, and walk in this holy Fear of the Lord so that our communities and nation can see the fullness of His Kingdom established.

> *Yes, if you call out for insight and raise your voice for understanding, if you seek it like silver and search for it as for hidden treasures, then you will understand the fear of the Lord and find the knowledge of God (Proverbs 2:3-5).*

Father, we pray that our hearts and minds would be pliable and usable for Your glory. We ask that You would come and overshadow us with Your holiness and Your might so that we would reflect Your glory on the earth. We give you permission to come and turn our hearts so that...

- We will show no fear toward evil but overcome it (see Isaiah 8:12-13).

- We will be open to the counsel of others (see Proverbs 1:7).

- We will be teachable (see Psalm 25:12).

- We will show no partiality and take no bribes (see Deuteronomy 10:17).

- We will not consider ourselves better than anyone else (see Philippians 2:3).

- Our mouths will be filled with good things (see Proverbs 16:9-13).

- We will hate all forms of evil (see Proverbs 8:13).

- We will operate in wisdom and humility (see Proverbs 15:33).

- We will have true judgments by the Spirit and not by people (see Isaiah 11:3-4).

- We will love God's truths (see Psalm 112:1).

- Our house will be in order (see Psalm 128:1-4).

- We will show the fruit of riches, honor, and life (see Proverbs 22:4).

- We will walk in obedience to God's commands (see Psalm 86:11).

- We will let no sin rule over us (see Psalm 119:133).

- We will have no fear of man, but walk in the Fear of the Lord (see Proverbs 29:25).

- We will rule with justice, counsel, and might (see Isaiah 11:2-4).

> *Father, may we be conduits and vessels of honor to demonstrate and model the Fear of the Lord to those walking in darkness and the terror of the enemy. May we be examples of Your holiness and awe, exhibiting strength, valor, and favor with heaven to accomplish great things for Your Kingdom. For Your glory, alone. Amen.*

Prayer Declarations Over Our Leaders

As a prophetic declaration in alignment with heaven's charge, we can say this prayer on behalf of those whom the Lord has called into positions of influence and authority. Declare these promises over specific leaders which the Holy Spirit highlights.

- *Rule in the midst of your enemies!* Do not waver or back down! Stand in the face of opposition, knowing that all of heaven is with you (see Ephesians 6:13)!

- Do not fix your eyes on what is seen, but on what is unseen, for what is seen is temporary, but what is unseen is eternal (see 2 Corinthians 4:18)!

- Walk in the Fear of the Lord and the power of His might (see Micah 3:8)!

- Use your God-given authority to execute justice and establish righteous rule in the land (see Genesis 49:10; Psalm 60:7)!

- Rejoice in the Word of God which brings life and liberty to all who obey it (see Proverbs 10:29-32)!

- Your faithfulness to God will bring forth an inheritance and eternal reward that no one can match. As you represent the King and carry His heart for the nation, be anointed with the oil of gladness and joy beyond your companions so that all may see He alone is God (see Psalm 45:6-7)!

- As you fear the Lord, He will instruct you in the way that you should choose. Your soul shall abide in well-being, and your offspring shall inherit the land. The friendship of the Lord is for you who fear Him, and He makes known to you His covenant for His name's sake (see Psalm 25:12-14). All glory to the Father, both now and forevermore. Amen!

Chapter 3

The RISING EKKLESIA *and* KINGDOM AUTHORITY

What Is God's Government?

Go therefore and make disciples of all nations, baptizing them in the name of the Father and of the Son and of the Holy Spirit (Matthew 28:19).

For those who have been longing to be taken out of tribulation and be taken up before things get worse, I would urge you to consider our great commission. Rather than preparing to leave, we should be positioned to lead. Instead of predicting the end, we should be presenting our case. Rather than storing up provisions for fear of impending doom, we should be out in our communities releasing the clarity, purpose, and wisdom that our culture so desperately needs. Though Jesus clearly said to be ready for His return, His primary message was to preach the gospel, demonstrate the Kingdom, and bring order to the earth He gave us.

Good government rises and falls on leadership. This is true in both the sacred and secular realms. The dysfunctional leadership now in some of the highest positions of our government is, unfortunately, a reflection of the Church's dysfunctional leadership. This is not from lack of love for God or even love for others. It's due to immaturity of character, lack of accountability in leadership, and an incomplete theological framework for Kingdom expansion. The fatherless generation talked about for decades is now grown up and seeking positions of power and influence. Without a solid biblical worldview and community of faith in place, we will continue to see wicked rulers rise and Kingdom expression curtailed.

Government Was God's Idea

*For to us a child is born, to us a son is given; and the **government** shall be upon his shoulder, and his name shall be called Wonderful Counselor, Mighty God, Everlasting Father, Prince of Peace. Of the increase of his government and of **peace** there will be no end, on the throne of David and over his kingdom, to establish it and to uphold it with justice and with righteousness from this time forth and forevermore. The zeal of the Lord of hosts will do this* (Isaiah 9:6-7).

The word "government" in Isaiah is from the Hebrew word *misra* meaning "to prevail, have power, rule, and dominion." This governmental power and dominion flows from a Wonderful Counselor, Everlasting Father, and Prince of Peace, whose government is the first and the only government that will endure forever.

The major mark of God's government is *peace* (verse 7). He has established His Kingdom government so that man can live in peace with himself, his God, and his fellow man. God's government produces justice and right decisions to all who serve the King's purposes. It is always growing, producing life, and increasing in favor and blessing without end.

From the beginning of creation, God invited all people to be part of His government. He gave Adam and Eve the mandate to fill the earth, subdue it, and to have dominion over every living thing (see Genesis 1:28). He gave them the responsibility to steward all that He created. His plan was to always include His sons and daughters in ruling and reigning with Him on the earth.

In Mark 1:15, Jesus preached, *"The time is fulfilled, and the kingdom of God is at hand; repent and believe in the gospel."* The word "kingdom" is the Greek word *basileia,* meaning rule or dominion. The Kingdom is the government of God and is now at hand. It is a life-giving authority and rule that flows through the people of God to bring transformation to the earth. Jesus demonstrated this Kingdom and governmental authority by overturning the sentences of death and decay, and bringing life, alignment, and supernatural increase in every area of our existence. He released this same authority to us in order to demonstrate, influence, and disciple entire nations in this Kingdom reality to transform the failing systems of humankind.

On Earth as It Is in Heaven

Even in the heavenly realms, there is a government at work. In Ephesians 3:10, it speaks of the *"rulers and authorities in heavenly places."* Daniel 10:13 describes Michael, the archangel, as *"one of the chief princes"* among the heavenly host. Additional Scriptures allude to orders and ranks of heavenly beings (see Genesis 3:24; Isaiah 6:1-3; Ephesians 3:10; Colossians 1:16). God is truly the Creator of every governmental structure on both sides of the veil.

For by him all things were created, in heaven and on earth,
visible and invisible, whether thrones or dominions or rulers
or authorities—all things were created through him and for
him (Colossians 1:16).

The purpose of God's government is to reconcile to Himself all things
in both realms to bring peace to His creation. Ever since the fall of man,
God has been working to bring order back to the chaos and blessing
back from the curse. In His ultimate act of love, He gave His Son to
make the way possible. Now, He extends to His sons and daughters, the
invitation to partner with Him in rendering decisions that will restore
order and reconcile humankind to God, once and for all. This is what
heaven is doing and this is what His Kingdom governmental authority
accomplishes.

Jesus taught His disciples to pray that His Kingdom would come,
and His will would be done on earth as it is in heaven (see Matthew
6:10). This is an invitation for the government of God to be made manifest on the earth—with us as His ambassadors. That which is done in
the heavenly realms to bring divine order, liberty and freedom, abundant life, and the presence of the Holy One, is to be established here on
the earth.

The entire ministry of Jesus was a training ground for His followers to
learn what He modeled so we could replicate it for generations to come.
It not only included salvation along with signs, wonders, and miracles,
but the administration of the Spirit, and the building of the House of
the Lord from which all other mountains would seek truth and direction (see Isaiah 2:2). Our commission doesn't only include salvation, but
discipling nations to follow a heavenly pattern of Kingdom power and
authority.

Until we all attain to the unity of the faith and of the knowledge of the Son of God, to mature manhood, to the measure of the stature of the fullness of Christ (Ephesians 4:13).

Church Government Versus Secular Government

If we are to be effective ambassadors of His Kingdom and transformative change agents in our nation, we must distinguish God's government apart from the governments of the world. For too long, the Church has kept governmental affairs at arm's length and refused to engage, thinking it was only "secular." We have confused politics with government and missed our opportunity to impact and influence our culture in significant ways (see Jeremiah 29:7).

Without the Church engaging in governmental affairs, secular rulers will govern the land by default and legislate ungodly laws to silence our voice and deny us our commission. It is clear in Scripture that God has created government for the good of the people as well as the good of the gospel. When we understand the purpose of government in both the secular and sacred realms, we are better empowered to do our part in establishing righteous rule on the earth.

The mistake most Christians have made regarding secular government is that it is supposed to function like the Church. We have imposed our beliefs and expectations on government structures and leaders and wrongly assumed their roles and purpose. Whereas the Church's role is to preach the gospel and proclaim the Kingdom, the government's role is to preserve the peace by protecting the weak and punishing the wrong.

Let every person be subject to the governing authorities. For there is no authority except from God, and those that exist have been instituted by God. Therefore, whoever resists the authorities resists what God has appointed, and those who resist will incur judgment. For rulers are not a terror to good conduct, but to bad. Would you have no fear of the one who is in authority? Then do what is good, and you will receive his approval, for he is God's servant for your good. But if you do wrong, be afraid, for he does not bear the sword in vain. For he is the servant of God, an avenger who carries out God's wrath on the wrongdoer. Therefore, one must be in subjection, not only to avoid God's wrath but also for the sake of conscience. For because of this you also pay taxes, for the authorities are ministers of God, attending to this very thing. Pay to all what is owed to them: taxes to whom taxes are owed, revenue to whom revenue is owed, respect to whom respect is owed, honor to whom honor is owed (Romans 13:1-7).

In this passage, we are told that God has established all authorities and that we are to submit to them out of reverence for Him. The apostle Paul is speaking specifically here to *governing authorities* and not church leaders. He gives specific instructions regarding their God-given role, as well as our responsibility in obeying their rules.

God uses governing authorities to:

- Bring terror to those with bad conduct.

- Use the sword to punish and bring wrath on the wrongdoer.

- Collect taxes for the good of the people.

Our responsibility to these governing authorities is to:

- Submit to their leadership or resist God and incur judgment.

- Do what is good.

- Keep a clear conscience by paying taxes.

- Respect and honor those who are due.

The government's role is not to "turn the other cheek" or "extend mercy" to those who do wrong. Its job is to protect the innocent and punish those who threaten others. God has established "secular" government to rule *all* people—both saved and unsaved—in order to keep peace in the land. A government properly run will ensure that all people in the land are protected from those who seek to do harm.

To keep things in perspective, this was written when Emperor Nero was in power. The government of that day was evil and wicked. God's instructions were given at a time when the governing authorities were godless and self-serving. Even so, His instructions kept His people's hearts clear. The Kingdom principles of authority and submission were in play, regardless of the individual rulers or their motives. God's rule would prevail as long as His people remained pure of heart and free from offense.

> *Be subject for the Lord's sake to every human institution, whether it be to the emperor as supreme, or to governors as sent by Him to punish those who do evil and to praise those who do good. For this is the will of God, that by doing good you should put to silence the ignorance of foolish people. ...Servants, be subject to your masters with all respect, not only to the good and gentle but also to the unjust. For this is a gracious thing, when, mindful of God, one endures sorrows while suffering unjustly* (1 Peter 2:13-19).

These verses speak specifically to our attitudes toward authorities we deem to be unfair and cruel. Even when we don't like them, we are instructed to honor their role and office. Unless we are told to go directly against God's Word, we must abide by the laws of the land and the directives of our leaders. How we respond—even to wicked leaders—can be a demonstration of the unseen Kingdom whose influence and power supersedes all others.

In our current political climate, this is increasingly difficult for God-honoring believers who see those in power as corrupt and self-serving. We must remember that in the United States, politicians are elected by the people, thus putting the responsibility—or blame—squarely on our own shoulders. It has only been in recent years that Christians are waking to this reality and beginning to get more engaged in the electoral process to assure that God-honoring officials are elected—or removed.

However, in our attempt to redefine godly leadership, we cannot confuse the qualifications for governing authorities with church leaders. Scriptures, again, clarify these roles and what God expects of both types of leaders.

Church Leadership Versus Secular Leadership

Numerous passages in the New Testament detail the job descriptions and expectations for those chosen to lead the church. The long lists of character qualities, moral choices, and relational dynamics are given to ensure the purity of heart and truthful integrity of anyone considering a position of leadership within the Body of Christ.

We find these lists in First Timothy 3, Titus 1:6-9, and First Peter 5:1-3. Some of the expectations listed are as follows: being above reproach, temperate and self-controlled, respectable and hospitable, able to teach, a lover of good, upright, holy and disciplined, not given to drunkenness, not violent but gentle, not quarrelsome, not a lover of money, not a recent convert, having a good reputation with outsiders, able to give instruction in sound doctrine, able to keep their household and children in order, etc.

It is evident that those whom the Lord calls to lead the Church are held to a high standard. They, and their household, must demonstrate godly character and a life of integrity that upholds biblical values. Their role is to bring the lost into the Kingdom (see Matthew 18:16-20), disciple believers into holiness and godliness (see 1 Timothy 4:6-11), and to mature the Bride of Christ (see Ephesians 4:12-16).

However, the Bible refers to civil servants differently. Rather than a list of qualifications, Scriptures detail how God will use governmental leaders to accomplish His purposes. In Romans 13:1-6 and First Peter 2:13-14, the role of governing authorities within human institutions describes a different kind of leader. They are:

- *God's servant* for the good of the people

- *A terror* to bad conduct, bearing the sword

- *Avengers* who carry out God's wrath on the wrongdoer

- *Servants of God*, attending to taxation of the people

- *Sent by God to punish* those who do evil and *praise* those who do good

These job descriptions include no reference to personal morality or godliness. These civil authorities are used by God, and in that sense are authorized by Him, yet their personal conduct and behavior is not mentioned. Their primary role is to keep the people safe from harm, punish those who break the law, and reward those who do good. The authority granted to them is so strong that it should even bring *"terror"* to those who break the laws of the land.

In Exodus 18:21-22, judges were appointed to govern the people. Their list of qualifications called for men who feared God, were trustworthy, and hated bribes. Again, their personal morality was not a factor, as much as their track record of being truthful, honest and God-fearing. King Cyrus (see Isaiah 45) and the Pharaoh (see Genesis 41) were both heathen rulers, yet they recognized God at work and allowed the people of God to flourish and succeed. In both Testaments, God's purposes for governing rulers were to discern rightly, judge fairly, and follow the laws of the land so that all would thrive.

What does this mean in today's political process? As believers, we can certainly pray that all our elected officials would fear the Lord and love God. At the same time, there will be those who do not follow Christ, yet have made the personal choice to honor those who do. Unlike church leaders who must model Christ to the flock, civil government leaders must rule over many who are not yet saved and have no godly standard for righteous rule. This is what creates a society where believers can be free to exercise their faith and share the gospel without hindrance.

Let's not disqualify those whom the Lord chooses as civil authorities simply because they may not pass the litmus test for church leaders. Their roles are different as are their job descriptions. Even as we pray for our governing officials to have a life-changing encounter with Christ, let us also pray that they would meet the qualifications for governing well.

To summarize, these are the foundational truths concerning the government of God:

1. God created government, both in the natural and in the spirit, to bring reconciliation between God and humanity, and peace to the earth.

2. Jesus gave us authority to govern here on the earth, just as He does in heaven.

3. Secular governments have different roles than church governments, but both have their purpose in fulfilling Kingdom purposes.

4. The leadership roles of civil authorities and church authorities differ, but both have been authorized by God to bring peace and stability to those they serve.

Taking Dominion Where It Counts

When I speak of governing here on the earth, I am not referring to "taking dominion" in the way some in the Body of Christ have thought. Our rule is not one which seeks total domination over every institution on the earth or some zealous takeover of every mountain in culture. That's what the disciples in Jesus' day thought would happen. They didn't get it, either.

Kingdom rule is the reality of an unseen Kingdom at work in every sphere of our culture; bearing such weight, authority, and influence, it's impact is powerful and tangible. It will be felt by the implicit, supernatural authority that accompanies those who operate in it, bringing substantial results that are not possible through natural means. It is we, the ambassadors of heaven, who are the carriers of this Kingdom authority and those who bring heaven to earth in our various realms of influence. This is not necessarily by ruling over others in the natural as much as ruling and reigning in the spirit. We have the opportunity to bring this kind of impact to every mountain of our culture through our witness and righteous actions, regardless of our roles or positions.

God took Daniel to a governmental mountain in his day to bear heaven's authority with a heathen ruler. Joseph was made second in command to the Pharaoh of Egypt in order to save God's people from extinction. The apostle Paul was led into the courts of Caesar to make an appeal for the gospel. In each case, it was not an organized takeover or attempt at domination, but a living demonstration of Kingdom rule and authority that so impacted the pagan rulers of the day, God's people prospered, and the glory of the true King became known. They ruled in the midst of their enemies (see Psalm 110:1-2).

Regardless of our seats of authority in the natural realm, there is one place that we have been called to be seated and take dominion— in the spiritual realm. We are seated with Christ in heavenly places (see

Ephesians 2:6) in order to reign with Him, putting everything in subjection under His feet.

> *That he worked in Christ when he raised him from the dead and seated him at his right hand in the heavenly places, far above all rule and authority and power and dominion, and above every name that is named…. And he put all things under his feet and gave him as head over all things to the church, which is his body, the fullness of him who fills all in all* (Ephesians 1:20-23).

> *The Lord says to my Lord: "Sit at my right hand, until I make your enemies your footstool* (Psalm 110:1).

We know that our battle is not against humans, but against the rulers and authorities in the spiritual realms who are trying to steal, kill, and destroy our Kingdom authority. *This* is the place where we are to reign as sons and daughters of the King to take dominion and rule over every seat of darkness set against the Lord. As coheirs with Christ, we wrest the authority from illegal spiritual invaders over the Body of Christ and over our nation. It is here that our true authority is tested and matured so we have legitimate authority on the earth.

The kingdom of darkness will continue to press in, and the work of our adversary will never stop advancing until the final day of judgment. However, in the midst of that darkness, the light of Christ will shine, for *"Of the increase of his government and of peace there will be no end"* (Isaiah 9:7). Jesus' commission was for us to disciple His Bride among every nation of the earth to show forth the glory of His Father and demonstrate what heaven looks like. We do this by exercising our God-given authority in the spiritual realm first, thus impacting and shifting the authorities on the earth.

Executing Justice on the Earth

In late 2017 I was shown why it is so important for the Body of Christ to understand our spiritual authority in these days. Heaven is rendering God's justice on the earth and He has invited us as Kingdom agents to execute that justice through our prayers, proclamations, and righteous deeds.

> *I saw the region surrounding Washington, DC, and a platform that someone was standing on. It was in the midst of a vast ocean that was dark and swirling. I saw a huge gavel from heaven coming down from above, ready to strike the platform. I knew the one standing on the platform was unaware of the judgment coming. I needed to warn him.*
>
> *Those who saw from a distance avoided the crash of the gavel—the first time. Suddenly, an unexpected immense wall of water came from behind this platform, carrying another gavel. I saw it emerge from the depths, but this time, the **handle** of the gavel came directly to **me**—as if an invitation to take it—and use it. The force of the water was so great there was no avoiding the crush of the wave. Even so, the gavel had power over it. As I struggled to keep my head above the water, I felt something at my feet, as if a warning.*

God's judgments are being rendered concerning the platforms of humanity. The messages we speak and the alliances we keep, are being watched and weighed. God is letting us know that decisions are being made in heaven's court and we must warn those who do not yet see or understand the severity of their choices.

He is also extending to us on earth this same authority in rendering decisions on His behalf. We do this through our prayers, our proclamations, and our righteous walk and deeds. As we watch with Him from heavenly places and declare His Word concerning the affairs of man, our Kingdom authority in prayer will bring justice and breakthrough. Even so, He is issuing a warning concerning our walk. Just as I felt something at my feet in the dream, the enemy will go after our attempts at spreading the gospel and try to "pull us under" if we are not properly attached to the Body of Christ.

The godly legislation needed on the land starts in the heavens through prayer, then manifests on the earth through us. The government of God is at work through us and we can rejoice in the invitation to partner with heaven to see the fullness of His Kingdom come to earth.

> *Let the godly exult in glory; let them sing for joy on their beds. Let the high praises of God be in their throats and two-edged swords in their hands, to execute vengeance on the nations and punishments on the peoples, to bind their kings with chains and their nobles with fetters of iron, to execute on them the judgment written! This is honor for all His godly ones. Praise the Lord!* (Psalm 149:5-9)

PRAYER GUIDE

MAY GOD'S GOVERNMENT *Be* ESTABLISHED *on the* EARTH

The heavens are the Lord's heavens, but the earth He has given to the children of man (Psalm 115:16).

Pray that the Kingdom of God would be powerfully demonstrated through the laws of the land and those who govern.

> *Lord Jesus, we praise You for the victory You gained on the cross, thus giving us the right to rule and reign with You forever (see Psalm 8:5-6).*

> *We acknowledge that it is You alone who gives us the wisdom and right to decree what is just and govern with righteousness (see Proverbs 8:15-16).*

We thank You for defeating our enemies and making them a footstool for Your feet (see Hebrews 10:12-13).

We declare that even those who oppose Your ways will submit to Your lordship because of the power of Your might (see Psalm 18:39-40).

Grant your leaders and those running for office to see things as You do as they administrate from a Kingdom perspective (see Proverbs 21:15).

May the elected officials, both current and future, maintain a pure heart and clean hands so that the laws and decrees they make will represent the integrity and authority of heaven (see Psalm 24:3-6).

May they be strengthened with inner resolve and perseverance, even in the face of growing aggression and intimidation, so that Kingdom authority is fully established here on the earth (see Psalm 125:2-3a).

Father, may we represent You rightly and carry Your heart for this nation, anointed with the oil of gladness so that all may see that You alone are God (see Psalm 45:6-7). In Jesus' name. Amen.

Pray for church leaders and pastors to take a righteous stand, speak with clarity, and encourage believers to engage in the electoral process.

We praise You, God, for giving us a voice to declare Your truth. We lift up our pastors and church leaders who have been called to speak and declare Your Word. We pray for Your grace to abound in their lives so that they would have all sufficiency in all things (see 2 Corinthians 9:8).

We pray that from their mouths would come knowledge and understanding concerning the issues affecting this nation. Grant them keen insight into the principles of holiness and godliness that bring life and liberty to those who trust in You (see 1 Timothy 6:11-14).

We ask that You would be a shield about them to guard their course and protect their way. Give them understanding in what is right, just, and fair (see Ephesians 6:16).

We pray that wisdom will save them from the ways of the wicked and that Kingdom truths would be a joy to their soul (see Proverbs 2:6-12).

May they walk in the Fear of the Lord and be free from the fear of man (see Proverbs 29:25).

We pray for their testimony to be pure and their example uncompromised (see 1 Timothy 3:2-7).

May their witness inspire many and may they receive their full inheritance in You. For Your glory alone. Amen.

Chapter 4

ARE
We QUALIFIED
to RULE?

Not All Authority Is Equal

I f we have embraced the call to establish the mountain of the Lord and walk in the Fear of the Lord as Kingdom ambassadors, we must consider the personal cost of this call. We must prayerfully consider our readiness to step into this role of spiritual authority and all that it requires of us. Before we can operate in any corporate authority, we must understand our personal authority as believers as well as the role of spiritual authorities in the Church.

There is a desperate need to raise the standard for godly authority in the land. Many have become disillusioned with authority figures due to disappointments, betrayals, and lost trust. We need new models of leadership that are free from control, manipulation, and self-promotion, not only on national platforms, but behind church pulpits.

It is no longer enough to call for integrity and truth—it's time to demonstrate it. The only agency that has the lasting power and authority from heaven to change the way we govern and lead is the Church. It is we, the Body of Christ, who are to be set apart as examples of godly government. We are the ones uniquely called and empowered by the Lord to disciple nations toward healthy leadership and righteous rule.

The only problem is, we have our own issues with authority. The spirit of rebellion has spread to the Church as roots of bitterness have taken hold. Disappointed believers have left local congregations out of frustration with leadership and a growing distrust in ministry agendas. Negative church experiences with spiritually abusive pastors and unhealthy church systems have turned away many looking for a place to land. It has resulted in some bad theology and ungodly mindsets that are weakening the Body.

Until we understand the purpose and need for spiritual authority and get aligned with God's governmental order in His House, we will not be qualified to rule or able to cleanse and reform other authority structures in the land. Our success in demonstrating Kingdom leadership will only be as good as our theology and worldview, and only as healthy as our mindsets and attitudes.

On Whose Authority?

Scriptures tell us much about authority and the various ways we are influenced by it. God wants us to know who and what we answer to, and why. The checks and balances He has provided in His Word are not only principles for success, but also provide the appropriate boundaries for healthy leadership and accountability.

There are seven different "levels" of authority spoken of in Scripture that can help us prioritize our goals and shape our decisions. The first one is the most important source of authority and carries the greatest consequence or reward. As the list progresses, each level of authority submits to the authority preceding it, thus putting things in proper order of accountability.

God Himself

I know that you can do all things, and that no purpose of yours can be thwarted (Job 42:2).

God is the ultimate and perfect authority over all, sovereign and supreme. He is the same yesterday, today, and forever, and we can count on His steadfast love and overriding power to do what He intends.

God's Word

Do not think that I have come to abolish the Law or the Prophets; I have not come to abolish them but to fulfill them (Matthew 5:17).

The Word of God is the written account of His eternal law that is inspired, inerrant, and without fault concerning His intentions and purposes for us. Every principle needed to live a righteous life and fulfill our creation mandate is provided in Scripture.

These first two levels of spiritual authority never change. They are eternal and immutable. God's Word "submits" to His own heart and character, and both are foundational to any subsequent understanding of authority.

Our Conscience

For I am not aware of anything against myself, but I am not thereby acquitted. It is the Lord who judges me (1 Corinthians 4:4).

When fed properly by God's Word, our conscience, our "heart," holds us accountable to Truth. However, if we feed upon negative reports and false information, our conscience will be seared and unable to lead us rightly (see 1 Timothy 4:1-4). It is our God-given conscience that moves our hearts and helps us to know and follow God's will.

Delegated Authorities

Obey your leaders and submit to them, for they are keeping watch over your souls, as those who will have to give an account... (Hebrews 13:17).

God is the One who calls and appoints leaders (see Romans 13:1). In our government, citizens affirm that call by voting officials into office. Believers in the Church are also to recognize and affirm those whom God has called to serve in leadership. This is not dependent on their likability, but their commission. Unless we are told to go directly against the higher authority of God's Word, we must seek to respect their roles, pray for their success, and follow their leadership.

Contractual Authority

Now in earlier times in Israel, for the redemption and transfer of property to become final, one party took off his sandal and gave it to the other. This was the method of legalizing transactions in Israel (Ruth 4:7 NIV).

This kind of authority is given through a written contract, verbal agreement, vow, rental agreement, etc. When "under contract" we are obliged to adhere to the rules assigned in the contract for the time allotment given. We are called to honor its authority unless a higher authority releases us from the contract.

Positional Authority

Honor everyone. Love the brotherhood. Fear God. Honor the emperor (1 Peter 2:17).

This recognizes the various positions of authority that people carry by virtue of their office, responsibility, or age. We honor the office of president or pastor simply because of the weight each office carries. We honor military personnel, police and rescue, and other positions that are responsible for our safety and well-being. We honor the elderly out of respect for their journey and our parents because it pleases the Lord. Positional authority is honored and esteemed because of the responsibilities associated with it.

A Particular Gifting

For you can all prophesy one by one, so that all may learn and all be encouraged (1 Corinthians 14:31).

Spiritual gifts are given by the Holy Spirit as He chooses. When we recognize and honor the gifts in operation, we are recognizing the authority of the Holy Spirit in revealing the Father's heart and purpose. Where some would like to place this authority higher because of the supernatural aspect of a gift, it must always be tested through the filters of preceding authorities.

Other than the first two authorities of God Himself and His Word, which always outweigh the others, the rest may shift in order of priority depending on the situation. The principle to be learned is that there *is* a proper order of authority and accountability. We cannot place any "word of the Lord" above God's written Word if in question. Nor can we lower the role of delegated authorities simply because we do not agree with them. Each level of authority carries a purpose and has its place.

The Power of Divine Order

How does this understanding affect our ability to govern and rule? When the authorities in our lives are properly aligned, it brings the greatest blessing and the greatest outcome, both personally and corporately. It reminds us that our relationship with our heavenly Father is the only way to know the true nature of godly authority. This can only happen in intimate fellowship with Him on a consistent basis. Next, we must regularly feed on His Word in order to be in alignment with His statutes and His principles.

> *And if you faithfully obey the voice of the Lord your God, being careful to do all His commandments that I command you today, the Lord your God will set you high above all the nations of the earth* (Deuteronomy 28:1).

The spirit of rebellion actually turns these levels upside down. One who defies spiritual authority believes their own "gift" or experience carries more weight and authority, totally disregarding God, His Word, or any delegated authority figure. Without a change of heart and transformation of beliefs, those who walk in defiance will continue to fight in the dark with no clear path to follow.

Our understanding of spiritual authority will directly impact us personally in how we discern truth and fulfill our assignments. It will also greatly impact the way we pray and intercede for the authorities in the land. Without an alignment of our hearts and minds to God's divine order, we will pray without understanding and miss the mark. When we know God's governmental structure for authority and accountability, our prayers will align more perfectly to heaven's blueprint, our vision will be clear, and we can release greater blessing and favor upon those He has put in place.

It Starts with Personal Submission

One of the most important character qualities in effective intercession is humility and honoring authority. Before we can begin interceding for those in authority, we must deal with any personal experiences that are skewing or misinterpreting our perceptions. Our encounters with authority, both positive and negative, will greatly impact our discernment and response. Until we recognize and deal with the protective filters and any resulting ungodly mindsets, we will be handicapped in our prayers.

In the early years of my own leadership development, I had many struggles with spiritual authority. I grew up in a traditional conservative denomination and community that was not favorable to women leaders. This automatically placed me in a subservient role because of my gender. When my prophetic gifts began to emerge, it put even more pressure on my journey when church leaders would not recognize my gift or encourage my call. Even my husband struggled to understand how my gifts were to function alongside his role as a pastor. I felt alone, misunderstood, and ignored.

Through the years-long journey, I discovered that my wounds from growing up in an emotionally abusive home had placed filters on my eyes and over my heart, making it almost impossible to receive counsel or instruction from any spiritual authority in my life. It was only after going through a long process of inner healing and deliverance from religious and controlling spirits, I was free to see the real blessing and power of spiritual authority. Where I had kept the authority figures in my life at arm's length out of fear and self-protection, I learned to see the tremendous blessing of oversight and accountability in developing my gifts and maturing in my call.

My husband also had to deal with theological barriers concerning women in leadership and five-fold ministry gifts. Where I had seen his hesitation as a sign of manipulation and control, we learned it was primarily due to his lack of understanding in how the biblical principles pertaining to these issues were applied within a local congregation. Once he received the needed counsel from our apostolic leaders and prayerfully researched on his own, he came to a fresh revelation of what God was doing in our lives as a couple and as leaders. Where I had emotional wounds that needed healing, he had theological questions that needed answering. Thankfully, we both overcame our barriers and learned to celebrate God's design for government, both at home and in the Church.

Women, especially, struggle with the question of spiritual authority. Though there is no "one size fits all" approach, the principles of honor, mutual submission, and celebrating spiritual gifts should be a healthy starting point for any discussion (see 1 Peter 2:17; Ephesians 5:21; 1 Corinthians 12). I personally learned that even when a spiritual authority does not recognize my gift or call, my own responsibility in how I honor, pray for, and support them does not change. In fact, some of my greatest breakthroughs came when I humbled myself before leaders who didn't "see" me, and I trusted the Lord with any needed validation.

Being set free from the need to prove myself or my gifts cleansed my heart in unexpected ways. I realized that the posture of my heart toward spiritual authority was central to the effectiveness of my prayers. Because I had feared and resented the authorities in my own life, I had limited authority in my intercession for the Church.

Alignment with Authority
Brings Alignment in Prayer

Therefore, confess your sins to one another and pray for one another, that you may be healed. The prayer of a righteous person has great power as it is working (James 5:16).

This familiar passage talks about righteous prayers, but it is only in the context of healthy relationships that those prayers have effect. It is critical that intercessors have a proper heart toward authorities, both inside and outside the church. Any negative experiences from the past must be dealt with if there is to be any oneness of heart and corporate impact in the spirit.

I recognized that some of the "authority" I claimed to have in the early part of my journey was actually a self-promoting attitude seeking validation and approval. The sense of power I gained from Spirit-inspired intercession was ill-gotten as I sought to take control where I could. Because I felt that authorities in the natural would not listen to me, I seized the chance for heavenly authorities to hear my voice. I wanted to feel powerful; and when I couldn't get it from the pulpit, I pursued it in the prayer room.

Unfortunately, the adversary recognizes illegitimate authority and will disqualify our prayers if we are not healed and set free from past resentments and criticism toward our leaders. I had to repent for my underlying motivation and lay down any sense of entitlement. I determined to approach the throne of grace with much more humility and trust the Lord with my desire for Kingdom advancement. He was more than faithful as I grew to understand that it wasn't my recognition in the natural that brought breakthrough, but my humble heart and right standing with the Lord that brought heaven's favor and increase.

> ...*God opposes the proud but gives grace to the humble* (James 4:6).

Not All Authority Is Equal

Another misconception that many intercessors have about authority in prayer is that we have "all" spiritual authority over any realm and any circumstance. This is what influences much of the spiritual warfare movement in terms of our approach and attitude. However, I would like to suggest an upgrade to some of our beliefs and practices.

Through years of both teaching on prayer and watching the fruit from individual and corporate intercession, I have observed three different kinds of spiritual authority that we usually operate in: Granted, Gained, and Given. Rather than seeing all spiritual authority as equal, Scripture reveals ways in which these different kinds of authority are formed, who activates them, and the impact they can have.

Granted Authority

Granted authority is the authority that every believer is granted through the work of the cross.

> *In him we have redemption through his blood, the forgiveness of our trespasses, according to the riches of his grace* (Ephesians 1:7).

> *Bless the Lord, O my soul, and forget not all his benefits, who forgives all your iniquity, who heals all your diseases* (Psalm 103:2-3).

By virtue of this authority, we can rebuke all the works of the evil one in our own lives, in our families, and in our sphere of influence in our church or community. This is the authority that Jesus gave to us so that people can be free from demonic oppression and enemy attack.

> *And he called the twelve together and gave them power and authority over all demons and to cure diseases, and he sent them out to proclaim the kingdom of God and to heal* (Luke 9:1-2).

It is "ground-level" warfare because it touches the people we know and see. We did not earn this authority. It has been freely granted to us so that we can demonstrate the power of Christ's resurrection and the freedom available to all who are held captive. However, it is limited. It does not necessarily give us authority over regional principalities or territorial spirits. Those are corporate strongholds outside our personal realm of authority and must be prayerfully discerned in partnership with other believers and recognized spiritual authorities. (We will address this further in Chapter 9).

Gained Authority

Gained authority is the authority that grows out of a believer's walk of obedience, faithfulness, and perseverance in trial.

> *And Jesus, full of the Holy Spirit, returned from the Jordan and was led by the Spirit in the wilderness.... And Jesus returned in the power of the Spirit to Galilee...* (Luke 4:1,14).

When we have faithfully overcome a temptation and come out victorious after a wilderness experience, we have a new level of spiritual authority over that issue. If we have stood the test and been faithful to His Word, our discernment will sharpen, our faith will grow, and our boldness to confront evil will increase.

Even Jesus experienced this when He was led into the wilderness *"full"* of the Spirit but came out *"in the power"* of the Spirit. Because He faced His accuser and overcame His flesh as a man, He became filled with even greater spiritual authority that launched Him into His public ministry (see Mark 1:24-28). Just as Jesus demonstrated in His own ministry, this kind of authority continues to grow throughout our lifetime as we obey the Father's voice, persist in prayer, and overcome the attacks of the enemy.

Given Authority

Given authority is authority that can only be given to us by other recognized authorities, both in the natural and in the spirit.

> *So the Lord said to Moses, "Take Joshua the son of Nun, a man in whom is the Spirit, and lay your hand on him. Make him stand before Eleazar the priest and all the congregation, and you shall commission him in their sight. You shall invest him with some of your authority, that all the congregation of the people of Israel may obey"* (Numbers 27:18-20).

Even in the secular realm, we must be given proper authority to complete certain jobs or assignments. In like manner, our spiritual authority will increase when recognized spiritual authorities affirm us and commend our call, our gifts, and our anointing. Whether it's an assignment, a commission, ordination, or other recognition, our authority will shift and increase when spiritual leaders impart blessing and authority into our lives. God always works through honor and agreement. Just as we learn to honor those in authority over us, their recommendation upon us is just as powerful for our success.

For leaders called to a specific five-fold office or ministry mandate, there is often an initial personal encounter with the Lord that sets them apart with anointing and authority. Just as Moses was called and appointed at the burning bush, so God is still calling sons and daughters to miraculous journeys of faith through supernatural encounters and impartations of the Spirit. The fullest blessing and release, however, will come when those vessels of honor are properly recognized, blessed, and sent out from the Church as Kingdom ambassadors (see 1 Timothy 4:14 and Acts 15:32-33).

Qualified Authority Brings Tangible Results

The more we understand God's divine order of authority, both in the secular and the spiritual, we can properly align ourselves and pray effectively. If we want to see national strongholds uprooted and Kingdom authority established, we have to start at home. As we are faithful to walk alongside the authorities God has placed around us locally, praying for them and supporting them as He directs, God will entrust us with more. Though our authority in Christ is automatic through the cross, our authority in the land must be home-grown, tested, and matured. Let's pray that we are good stewards of this reality in order to become the transformative change agents this nation so desperately needs.

> *The one who conquers and who keeps my works until the end, to him I will give authority over the nations* (Revelation 2:26).

PRAYER GUIDE

ESTABLISHING GOD'S PEOPLE *in* HEAVEN'S AUTHORITY

1. Thank God for His appointed spiritual authorities, regardless of your personal opinions about them.

> *Let every person be subject to the governing authorities. For there is no authority except from God, and those that exist have been instituted by God. Therefore, whoever resists the authorities resists what God has appointed, and those who resist will incur judgment* (Romans 13:1-2).

2. Repent for any bitterness or resentment toward authority figures. Clear your heart of anything the enemy may use to disqualify your spiritual authority.

> *I will no longer talk much with you, for the ruler of this world is coming. He has no claim on me* (John 14:30).

...he was heard because of his reverent submission (Hebrews 5:7 NIV).

Therefore, confess your sins to one another and pray for one another, that you may be healed. The prayer of a righteous person has great power as it is working (James 5:16).

3. Ask for the Fear of the Lord to guard and guide your heart and mind.

And his delight shall be in the fear of the Lord. He shall not judge by what his eyes see, or decide disputes by what his ears hear (Isaiah 11:3).

4. Pray for the mind of Christ to establish truth and proper understanding. Determine to live by a higher standard than the world.

Do not be conformed to this world, but be transformed by the renewal of your mind, that by testing you may discern what is the will of God, what is good and acceptable and perfect (Romans 12:2).

But the wisdom from above is first pure, then peaceable, gentle, open to reason, full of mercy and good fruits, impartial and sincere (James 3:17).

5. Pray for obedient hearts that pursue holiness and righteousness above personal gain.

Strive for peace with everyone, and for the holiness without which no one will see the Lord (Hebrews 12:14).

See to it that no one takes you captive by philosophy and empty deceit, according to human tradition, according to the elemental spirits of the world, and not according to Christ (Colossians 2:8).

6. Pray that we would discern rightly and judge correctly with the Word of God.

If you abide in me, and my words abide in you, ask whatever you wish, and it will be done for you (John 15:7).

Teach me good discernment and knowledge, for I believe in Your commandments (Psalm 119:66 New American Standard Bible).

7. Ask that our hearts and prayers would be motivated by a God-given love for others.

And it is my prayer that your love may abound more and more, with knowledge and all discernment, so that you may approve what is excellent, and so be pure and blameless for the day of Christ (Philippians 1:9-10).

Above all, keep loving one another earnestly, since love covers a multitude of sins (1 Peter 4:8).

8. Pray for proper alignment with God's appointed leadership and agreement with the witness of the Body of Christ.

...Every matter must be established by the testimony of two or three witnesses (2 Corinthians 13:1 NIV).

Remind them to be submissive to rulers and authorities, to be obedient, to be ready for every good work, to speak evil of no one, to avoid quarreling, to be gentle, and to show perfect courtesy toward all people (Titus 3:1-2).

I appeal to you, brothers, by the name of our Lord Jesus Christ, that all of you agree, and that there be no divisions among you, but that you be united in the same mind and the same judgment (1 Corinthians 1:10).

9. Pray that believers would grow through their trials and gain greater depth of insight into the spiritual realm and God's Kingdom purposes on the earth.

But solid food is for the mature, for those who have their powers of discernment trained by constant practice to distinguish good from evil (Hebrews 5:14).

I write to you, fathers, because you know him who is from the beginning. I write to you, young men, because you are strong, and the word of God abides in you, and you have overcome the evil one (1 John 2:14).

10. Pray that our lessons learned would result in tangible evidence of the unseen realm and the glorious Kingdom of God.

My message and my preaching were not with wise and persuasive words, but with a demonstration of the Spirit's power (1 Corinthians 2:4 NIV).

You did not choose me, but I chose you and appointed you that you should go and bear fruit and that your fruit should abide, so that whatever you ask the Father in my name, he may give it to you (John 15:16).

Chapter 5

RIGHTEOUS RULE MUST *Be* MODELED

A Charge to Pastors

I grew up as a pastor's kid. Our journey as a family was filled with many heartaches, disappointments, and constant change. I said for years I wouldn't marry a pastor—and I didn't. Bobby was a sales representative for a local manufacturing company when we said our vows in 1988. Only God knew that within a year of getting married, Bobby would be called into full-time pastoral ministry. I can still see the smile on God's face when I realized how He had set us both up. It became evident that He had a purpose beyond our own human reasoning and bigger than our limited understanding.

Being married to a pastor now for more than thirty years has given me a unique perspective. Though I understand and grieve for many who have had negative experiences in church and are critical of pastoral leadership, I live behind the scenes and understand the pressures and pitfalls, as well as the potential for amazing good. I see the growing rift between the pew and the pulpit. Healing is needed on both sides if we are to come into proper alignment and oneness of heart. It must start with a proper understanding of the call on pastors and the charge we have been given to work together for Kingdom expansion.

Heaven Weeps for Pastors and Cries Out for Fathers

I woke up weeping. In my dream, the Lord showed me the heart of true pastors and their critical need for prayer. Their call is not to be char-ismatic CEOs of ministries, but spiritual fathers and mothers who shep-herd the flock. The grace on their lives is irreplaceable at a time when the lost and wandering sheep need a place to call home.

I saw two different pastors in two different settings. The first pastor was dressed in his sacred garments talking to a TV camera. He was walking around his office talking about the latest church campaign. He was laying out the professionally made and well-coordinated materials to go along with this initiative, urging the viewers to join in the program. I was impressed by his talent and charisma, but was not moved in my heart or my spirit.

Next, I was in a boardroom of a church and the members were sitting around the table processing a sad and painful transition. Sitting across from me was their pastor. I immediately knew in the spirit his heart for his flock. He was a true father. Humble of spirit, gentle, and compassionate. But, he was leaving. The members were grieving and at a loss. One even looked at me and said, "Do you really know him?" It was a statement more than a question. He was speaking to the quality of this man who had been their spiritual father and loving shepherd. As I looked around the table, I felt the sense of hopelessness. Though there were others who could take charge, they could not care for the people the way this pastor had. I began to cry and felt the deep pain of heaven at the depth of this loss.

Two dreams and two different scenarios. One pastor was producing growth through marketing strategies and mass appeals. His charismatic persona was captivating, but the authentic presence and power of the Holy Spirit was sorely lacking. The other pastor was a true shepherd at heart, but he was leaving his flock. Those who knew him felt the weight of his departure and I could feel the sense of loss. Regardless of the impressive talents or gifts of other leaders around the table, it was evident this devoted spiritual father could not be easily replaced. I woke up feeling the grief of heaven over a fading gift that is being lost in today's Church.

Being a pastor is not only costly on a personal level, but high-risk on the corporate level. The immense expectations from others can drive many leaders to succumb to a cultural mindset instead of a Kingdom one. In an effort to be relevant and successful in the eyes of others, some pastors find themselves compromising values and lowering the standard for a sanctified life in order to appease the crowds. For some it is their own insecurity and need for applause that takes them down this path. For others, the pressure to conform draws them into decisions based more on the fear of man than on the Fear of the Lord. Still others, like the pastor in my dream, feel inadequate in meeting the growing needs and expectations of a technologically driven generation.

These are very real and present dangers that are threatening our unity, our commission, and our call as the Body of Christ. If we want to pray effectively for the Church and how we impact our culture, we must consider the role of pastoral leadership in today's Church. It is only as we are better informed of God's blueprint for Kingdom rule in a community of believers that our prayers will be targeted and effective.

I believe there are several mindsets that must shift in order for the Ekklesia to take its place as a transformative change agent in this nation.

1. We must revisit our understanding of leadership roles within the church.

2. We must learn the God-given grace of pastors standing behind America's pulpits to better support and pray for them.

3. We must be convinced of the Church's role and voice in our nation's government.

Each of these strategic needs must be brought before the Lord in prayer. We must also determine to change our attitudes and upgrade our practices if we are to see the long-term results we long for.

New Testament Leadership Roles

The primary governing role in the early Church was given to elders in partnership with the apostles (see Acts 15:1-6, 22-23; 1 Timothy 5:17; Titus 1:5). It was the elders who were appointed in every city to watch over and care for the Church. In addition, Jesus gave other gifted leaders to supplement this work both locally and translocally. Whereas the elders served locally in a governing role, the "five-fold" leaders were responsible for equipping and empowering the people for extending the Kingdom.

> *And he gave the apostles, the prophets, the evangelists, the shepherds and teachers, to equip the saints for the work of ministry, for building up the body of Christ, until we all attain to the unity of the faith and of the knowledge of the Son of God, to mature manhood, to the measure of the stature of the fullness of Christ* (Ephesians 4:11-13).

Each of these five-fold ministers are specifically called to disciple and empower believers toward maturity, fruitfulness, and multiplication. Theirs is not a platform ministry as much as an equipping ministry. Their God-given mandate is not to grow a ministry, but to grow disciples.

This is where we have erred as a corporate Church in placing too much emphasis on the platform and not enough on the people. Jesus gave these ministers as gifts to the Church to train the saints to do the work of the ministry—not just pay someone else to work the fields. Though there are five-fold ministers in every sphere and mountain of our culture, I will speak specifically to the five-fold ministry within the Church.

The label "pastor" is often self-defeating. We have followed cultural precedent more than biblical protocol in using that term for a senior leader of a congregation. The term "pastor" is only used once in the New Testament in the New International Version (NIV) translation. It is better translated as "shepherd," which means to guard, protect, and care for the flock. Their job description, based on this passage, indicates they are one of the five equipping gifts, not necessarily a governing role. (Some suggest that the "shepherds and teachers" distinction is a single gift and not two separate gifts.) Following this pattern throughout the New Testament, one can see the role of elders, along with the apostles and prophets, providing needed direction, administration, and counsel to the church, with the other ministry gifts (evangelist, teacher, pastor) collaborating. Deacons are also mentioned as serving in a leadership capacity (see 1 Timothy 3:12).

Today, there are numerous kinds of church governments, some more closely aligned to the early Church and others not. In our own church network—DOVE International—we embrace the New Testament pattern and have an elder team in place as the governing authority in the church, with my husband being the "lead elder." He just happens to be a five-fold pastor, so his title of "Pastor Bobby" fits him well.

In many cases, however, a senior leader in today's church may not operate in the grace of pastor as much as a teacher or evangelist. Others serve more apostolically through their team-building and visionary leadership. Still others are prophetically motivated, focusing primarily on the gifts and works of the Holy Spirit. Yet, we call everyone a pastor by default. This can place undue pressure on some of these leaders when asked to deliver something outside their strength and realm of grace (see Romans 12:3).

Through following New Testament patterns and observing the fruit, we see some general characteristics concerning these five roles and functions:

- *Apostles GOVERN* – They are builders and pioneers, championing teamwork and vision. (See 1 Corinthians 4:14-17.)

- *Prophets GUIDE* – They give direction and vision through insight and foresight. (See Acts 11:28.)

- *Evangelists GATHER* – They stir up the Body to reach the lost with passion and power. (See Acts 8:5-6.)

- *Pastors GUARD* – They disciple, nurture, and mentor sons and daughters to bring the spiritual family to maturity. (See First Peter 5:1-2.)

- *Teachers GROUND* – They bring revelatory truth from Scripture to stabilize our faith. (See Acts 11:18.)

Because the Church has lacked a basic framework of these roles and functions, our personal needs and corporate expectations have misplaced our grievances. We have expected prophets to be more pastoral in their approach and teachers to be more prophetic in their message. We have complained when evangelists don't go deeper in the Word when their primary mandate is to reach the lost. We have been frustrated that prophets don't provide more personal care when their priority must be in the secret place. And, we have become indignant when pastors don't boldly challenge the status quo, when their primary call is to care for the sheep.

And I will give you shepherds after my own heart, who will feed you with knowledge and understanding (Jeremiah 3:15, 23:4).

These are probably gross generalities, but the point is that we must learn to recognize these five-fold ministers and the unique and specific call on their lives. Though most senior leaders within local congregations will probably continue to be labeled "pastor," we can still gain a deeper appreciation for each leader as we understand their biblical context.

It is not their title that qualifies them, but their favor and their fruit. Depending on the grace given them, their motivation, passion, and fruitfulness will be most effective when they focus on their strength and not their weakness. Through each unique gift, God desires to build, strengthen, and expand our Kingdom influence and impact on the earth. If we can learn to celebrate the God-given strengths of each gift and commend their unique contributions, our teams will be much stronger, our leadership more effective, and our voice more coherent.

The great need for the Church to speak out about issues of faith and morality is facing some challenges. For those senior leaders who carry a prophetic or teaching gift, confronting these issues with boldness and clarity comes more "naturally." However, it is a bit foreboding for the five-fold pastor who is more focused on calming the waves than on stirring up the waters. Their challenge will be to partner with other five-fold ministers in their communities to raise a standard of truth. Pastors can celebrate and engage those called to speak boldly on issues of the day without fearing division within the ranks. It will be through healthy relationships and a corporate vision that leaders can work together for the common good.

The dream I had about these two pastors illustrates the need for us as believers to remember and celebrate the much-needed role of pastors in today's culture. Though they may not always trumpet a prophetic charge to their congregations, their role is vital. Each of the five-fold ministers have visionary perspective and a desire to empower believers, but a pastoral leader carries the heart of a father or mother that is graced to do the necessary discipleship, mentoring, and training with tomorrow's leaders. If we want to see the next generation rise up with Kingdom influence in the various mountains of culture, someone will need to guide, pray with, and walk alongside these sons and daughters to ensure their success.

> *For though you have countless guides in Christ, you do not have many fathers...* (1 Corinthians 4:15).

This value is something sorely lacking in today's pop-church mentality that seeks instant influence and viral success. We have traded meaningful relationships and one-on-one discipleship for big-name recognition and crowd-filled auditoriums. It is no wonder that there are more rising religious stars pursuing the platform than there are rising servant leaders headed to the prayer room and fellowship hall.

The reality is that the changes we are praying for in the governmental realm can only happen with the support, prayers, and leadership of local congregations. Regardless of the national voices speaking out, local leaders need to find their own voice and set the standard at home. They must partner together, each using their unique gift and strength, to formulate a clear message to those in their own community. They are the ones to secure their own city for the Kingdom and disciple their followers to understand and apply these truths in the various spheres of influence in their own region.

Note: For the sake of cultural relevance, I will continue to use the term "pastor" for those who are senior leaders in the church.

Prophetic Charge to Pastors

With all wicked deception for those who are perishing, because they refused to love the truth and so be saved. Therefore God sends them a strong delusion, so that they may believe what is false, in order that all may be condemned who did not believe the truth but had pleasure in unrighteousness (2 Thessalonians 2:10-12).

The balance between preaching the Word of God and not offending the sheep is increasingly challenging. The divisive issues being addressed in our nation are forcing us to make hard choices. Do we stand on the unchanging standards of Scripture, or do we compromise the message, thinking we are appealing to more people?

The Lord showed me the cost of this battle through another dream. It should serve as a warning to pastors who don't recognize the enemy's agenda in hijacking the pulpit and the voice of the Church. The first scene indicated what God is doing through the next generation concerning the coming harvest. The second scene showed how some pastors are misinterpreting the spiritual battles behind the political agendas and falling into a trap.

> *I saw a young man paint a beautiful mural on the side of a building in his city. It was a modern-day proverb that drew attention from everyone in the community due to its profound message and creative expression. As I was watching, I knew in my spirit it was revealing Christ! Though not promoted as a "Christian" message, the underlying message was giving glory to the Creator Himself. A woman beside me, a nonbeliever, was also struck with the message and was greatly stirred. She even asked me, "Is this God!?" I was amazed how this fresh expression of the gospel had power to reach the lost.*

> *Next, I saw a pastor. He was standing at the foot of the steps to the city courthouse, getting ready to make a speech. He was wearing a cleric's robe and was excited about this opportunity to address his community. I caught him to tell him how excited I was about this amazing open door to preach the gospel and point people to God. But this pastor, whom I knew, was not "himself." He had a crazed look in his eyes and seemed to be highly distracted by all the attention from the crowd. Not only was he speaking gibberish, but he was very effeminate. He acted like someone else entirely and wasn't even listening to me. Instead of preparing to share the gospel with those who had been stirred by their hunger, this man of God was now a delusional performer preparing for the spotlight. As I saw him turn to give his speech, I woke up grieving in my spirit for this lost opportunity.*

Due to the prayers of many, this next generation is being drawn by the Spirit to express and reveal Christ to the unsaved in ways we have never seen before. The Spirit of God is hovering over the land and providing many divine appointments to reveal the glory of God to those who are searching. Praise God! And yet, the pastor in this dream isn't even in his right mind. He no longer saw reality through spiritual eyes, but through the eyes of the world. This warning to pastors is sobering.

If church leaders compromise the Word of God for a lie and give in to the crowds who want an excuse to sin, not only will these leaders become blind to what God is doing, they will lose touch with eternity's plan and totally miss the coming harvest of souls. They will miss this window of opportunity; but worse yet, they themselves will become delusional in their thinking and become a pawn in the enemy's hand.

It is not an accident that the pastor in the dream looked and acted like a female. Though people through the generations have always dealt with sin, it wasn't until our nation began to embrace homosexuality that we began to experience all other forms of evil.

> *Therefore God gave them over in the sinful desires of their hearts to sexual impurity for the degrading of their bodies with one another. They exchanged the truth about God for a lie, and worshiped and served created things rather than the Creator.... Furthermore, just as they did not think it worthwhile to retain the knowledge of God, so God gave them over to a depraved mind, so that they do what ought not to be done* (Romans 1:24-25,28 NIV).

One of the goals behind this demonic spirit is to strip men of their God-given authority as fathers to a fatherless generation. If they can be emotionally neutered and stripped of their identity in Christ, their authority will be greatly diminished. If the Church continues to embrace this kind of compromised lifestyle, we will reap the consequences from a host of other evils. We must pray that the Father's love can be extended through our kindness in order to bring them to repentance. We must realize the bondage they are in if we are to help set them free.

> *These are waterless springs and mists driven by a storm. For them the gloom of utter darkness has been reserved. For, speaking loud boasts of folly, they entice by sensual passions of the flesh those who are barely escaping from those who live in error. They promise them freedom, but they themselves are slaves of corruption. For whatever overcomes a person, to that he is enslaved* (2 Peter 2:17-19).

The call is clear. We must pray for our pastors and those who lead congregations in our local communities. The fact that the pastor in the dream was standing in front of the courthouse indicates the spiritual authority that God has given the shepherds (see Jeremiah 3:15). They are to be the voices in local communities as moral compasses and champions of righteousness! We must pray for them to be faithful to this call and not give in to the fear of man.

Pastors and Politics

Many pastors are reluctant to talk about political issues in their churches because of the potential backlash from members. The fear of losing congregants or financial support is an underlying concern for many church leaders when addressing controversial topics. There are also those who believe that legislative issues and governing policies have no place in church life. However, we must separate politics from government and wrestle with some serious questions:

- Is it possible for the Church to be a unified voice in the public square on relevant issues?

- Is it possible for believers to agree on the Word of God concerning critical legislative issues?

- Is it possible for pastors to empower their congregations without getting politically divisive?

In our 25-plus years of pastoral ministry, we have wrestled with these same questions. Yet, we have learned to empower our congregation from a Kingdom perspective and not a worldly one. Rather than addressing political differences, our goal is to provide a solid biblical foundation from which believers can build a proper understanding of biblical morals and values, godly government, and Kingdom practices.

Where in previous decades we didn't see morality being legislated in this nation, we are now seeing elected officials passing laws and bills that not only censor our voices as believers but force us to join in practices that go directly against God's Word. It is no longer an option for pastors to distance themselves. Without the clarity from God's Word and practical wisdom to empower believers, we will have no foundation to stand on and no message with any power.

> *If a kingdom is divided against itself, that kingdom cannot stand. If a house is divided against itself, that house cannot stand* (Mark 3:24-25 NIV).

To help church leaders navigate the stirred-up waters of moral, social, and racial challenges in society, the following are some of the core values we have gleaned through the years in addressing legislative issues in the church:

> *As Christians, we can be governmental without being political (see Isaiah 9:7).*

God created government to establish order, starting with the first family in Genesis (see Genesis 1:26-28). It is a biblical principle of stewardship and order (see Proverbs 8:14-16). Politics, not mentioned in Scripture, is man's activities within government and focuses more on party preferences than on collective values.

> *Laws of the land determine the level of freedom believers have in sharing the gospel (see 1 Peter 2:13-14).*

We may have strong biblical convictions concerning our faith practices, but without laws supporting those beliefs and values, our Christian witness will be greatly hindered and limited. Our elected officials make those laws that we are legally bound to obey.

The Church is accountable to the Lord for our collective witness (see Micah 5:15).

When believers take part in the electoral process, we are being faithful stewards and responsible citizens (see Romans 13:5-7). We can bring positive change to our nation by electing officials who are God-fearing and God-appointed (see Romans 13:1). If we don't, we have relinquished our God-given role to nonbelievers by default.

We equip believers with the principles of God's Word and a Kingdom mindset.

Living out our faith in the public square is essential to our witness and demonstration of Kingdom values. Addressing issues based on scriptural truths empowers believers in their walk and strengthens our testimony.

We vote according to biblical values, not political parties (see Matthew 6:10).

Our standard for truth, life, and liberty is based on God's Word. We pray for all government leaders regardless of political party, but vote for candidates who support and uphold biblical values that are core to the Christian faith. Some of the most critical values would be the sanctity of life, biblical sexuality in traditional marriage, and religious freedom.

Even though pastors cannot endorse any specific candidate, they can preach the Word of God as it pertains to various issues. Thus, any disagreement that comes will be based on disagreeing with God's Word, not political platforms. Coming from a Kingdom mindset can enable pastors to lead effectively and provide the needed direction the Church desperately needs.

We are being tested as a Church in this process. Will we engage with the world we have been commissioned to reach concerning the issues that matter to them? Can we declare the Word of God with courage, demonstrating the same authority that Jesus had when He spoke of His Father's Kingdom? Will we stand with our pastors and church leaders when they speak up for righteousness? Prayer is the starting point but should result in a unified voice from the Church and a bold proclamation of the Kingdom of God.

> So then you are no longer strangers and aliens, but you are fellow citizens with the saints and members of the household of God, built on the foundation of the apostles and prophets, Christ Jesus himself being the cornerstone (Ephesians 2:19-20).

PRAYER GUIDE

For Pastoral Leadership *in the* Nation

1. Pray for God to move on pastors and church leaders to know and walk in the Fear of the Lord.

We ask that the Spirit of the Lord would rest upon each of them; the Spirit of wisdom and of understanding, the Spirit of counsel and of might, the Spirit of the knowledge and fear of the Lord (see Isaiah 11:1-2).

We pray that they would be aware and cognizant of Your presence and Your Kingdom rule (see Jeremiah 9:23-24).

We pray that they would make every effort to make their calling and election sure, knowing that they must ultimately answer to You for their choices and their witness (see 2 Peter 1:10).

May they be free from the fear of man so that they can follow Your voice and Your ways (see Proverbs 29:25).

May they acknowledge their need for Your grace, knowing that their works are dead without You (see 2 Timothy 1:9).

We pray that those whom You have specifically called in this hour would persevere in the midst of trials or setbacks and press on toward the goal to win the prize for which You have called them (see Philippians 3:13-14).

2. **Pray that those leading churches would have godly discernment to know what is good and right in the eyes of the Lord.**

May they not judge things according to how the world judges but choose to decide with the eyes and ears of the Spirit (see Isaiah 11:3-4).

May they walk in righteousness without stumbling (see Hosea 14:9).

May they have a renewed mind to be able to test and approve what Your will is—Your good, pleasing, and perfect will (see Romans 12:2).

May they distinguish good from evil and practice daily discernment (see Hebrews 5:14).

Fix their eyes on what is unseen in order to make sense of what is seen (see 2 Corinthians 4:18).

3. Pray that integrity and righteous government would be restored to church leadership.

Guard those who walk in integrity and may those who walk in unrighteousness be overthrown (see Proverbs 13:6).

Thank God for setting the righteous in His presence, enabling them to triumph over their enemies, and overshadow them in their call (see Psalm 41:11-12).

Pray that they would give careful thought to their steps and the paths before them. May they keep their feet from evil and may they stick to the road God has marked out for them (see Proverbs 4:25-27).

May they be honest in their financial dealings and honoring in their relationships (see Romans 13:7).

May they keep a clear conscience so that those who speak maliciously against their good behavior in Christ would be ashamed of their slander (see 1 Peter 3:16).

May the light of the righteous shine brightly, but the lamp of the wicked be snuffed out (see Proverbs 13:9). In Jesus' name. Amen.

Chapter 6

THE WORD *and the*
SPIRIT COMING
TOGETHER

Apostolic Authority and Prophetic Power

U ntil we feel a divine jealousy over His Body, we will never be properly motivated to guard, protect, and contend for our unity. Many are walking away from the Church, or wandering from church to church with negative attitudes and bitter words, causing mistrust, criticism, and isolation. Regardless of the reasons, we need to realize the damage done when we sentence the entire Church to a time-out because of the mistakes of a few.

> *Strive for peace with everyone, and for the holiness without which no one will see the Lord. See to it that no one fails to obtain the grace of God; that no "root of bitterness" springs up and causes trouble, and by it many become defiled* (Hebrews 12:14-15).

Our Corporate Identity

...as Christ loved the church and gave himself up for her, that he might sanctify her, having cleansed her by the washing of water with the word, so that he might present the church [Ekklesia] *to himself in splendor, without spot or wrinkle or any such thing, that she might be holy and without blemish* (Ephesians 5:25-27).

Jesus died to save us as individuals, but He is returning for us as a Bride. We are each responsible for our personal holiness, but we are corporately responsible for our sanctification as a Bride worthy of the Bridegroom. We are on a journey much bigger than our individual goals and aspirations. We must be joined together for a Kingdom cause that far outweighs our individual preferences or personal agendas. Somehow, we must find the same love for the Church that Christ has.

And walk in love, as Christ loved us and gave himself up for us, a fragrant offering and sacrifice to God (Ephesians 5:2).

To take down the demonic ruling authorities over our nation, we must have corporate authority. We cannot have corporate authority if we are divided or live in isolation. Unless we walk together and learn to work through our conflicts and differences, we will be handicapped in our prayers and have no standing in the spirit. We don't have to agree on everything, but we do need a love for the Church that can see past one another's flaws and mistakes.

It's one thing to leave a church because it doesn't align with your beliefs; it's another to slander a church because they don't do things according to your personal preference. Even when there is sin in the camp and need for accountability, we can walk through it with integrity, looking for ways to address the individuals while protecting our corporate witness (see Matthew 18:15-17).

As a community pastor, my husband teaches a quarterly class for visitors and newcomers who want to learn more about our church. A few years ago, he added a new subject that very few pastors would probably address: How to Leave a Church with Blessing. With the growing number of people coming through our doors, broken and bitter from previous church experiences, he wanted to empower people to make these transitions in a way that was honoring to God and protected the witness of the corporate Church in our community.

Many times, disgruntled prodigals move on to other congregations; and we have learned that how they leave one church is how they will enter the next. A negative testimony of any previous church or pastor will follow them. Without proper resolution, it's only a matter of time before that same testimony is repeated in the next stop on a person's church-hopping journey.

When we realize that the Church is much larger than any one congregation, and that we are all interconnected, we will guard our testimony and honor those in leadership, even when we disagree with them. It's Christ's Body we're talking about and He has a jealous love for it—*all* of it.

> *...But God has so composed the body, giving greater honor to the part that lacked it, that there may be no division in the body, but that the members may have the same care for one another. If one member suffers, all suffer together; if one member is honored, all rejoice together* (1 Corinthians 12:24-26).

Even in the worst of circumstances, we have learned you can leave a fellowship without destroying the Body. Bobby and I have our own testimony of unexpectedly leaving a church that I helped plant in my late twenties. After thirteen years of serving in leadership, our vision for ministry was at odds with the senior leader and we knew we couldn't stay. The transition out was a year-long process filled with many challenges. But, through a prophetic word the Lord had spoken to us, we knew that this transition would mark our next assignment. We took the time needed to work through the differences with prayerful communication, relational integrity, and personal humility. Even though there were numerous setbacks, misunderstandings, and opportunities for offense, we were able to leave with our relationships intact and a blessing from our oversight.

Though the process was personally painful, we were determined to honor the Body of Christ. We knew people were watching and felt the responsibility of stewarding the transition for a greater Kingdom purpose. That blessing was imprinted on our next church plant in a neighboring city. Within a few months of our new assignment, God's favor opened unusual doors to relationships with pastors and leaders in the community that brought us increased influence in the city. It also marked our congregation with a special healing grace to prodigals and orphans. Through the years we have ministered to many broken pastors and lost sheep looking for a place to heal.

We have personally seen the power of confronting conflicts in a godly way that not only brings blessing, but opens the door for God to intervene in ways we can't. We can honor the role we each play, bless our God-given strengths, and cover the weaker parts. Doing so honors the Lord; and when we honor Him, He honors us.

Rather than expecting to find one congregation that meets all our needs, we need to see that each congregation is but one expression of the larger Body of Christ within a community. Each fellowship has a role to play and gifts to offer. How we walk together as a city church will impact our intercession on behalf of the city. If we are to rise as a sanctified, empowered, and victorious Ekklesia, we need a zealous love to protect each other, care for one another, champion each other, and work as one toward a higher call. It is our responsibility to build up the Body and make ourselves ready for the Bridegroom.

Rather, speaking the truth in love, we are to grow up in every way into him who is the head, into Christ, from whom the whole body, joined and held together by every joint with which it is equipped, when each part is working properly, makes the body grow so that it builds itself up in love (Ephesians 4:15-16).

Apostolic Authority and Prophetic Power

If we are to build a healthy Body, we must also have the proper foundation to build upon.

So then you are no longer strangers and aliens, but you are fellow citizens with the saints and members of the household of God, built on the foundation of the apostles and prophets, Christ Jesus himself being the cornerstone, in whom the whole structure, being joined together, grows into a holy temple in the Lord. In him you also are being built together into a dwelling place for God by the Spirit (Ephesians 2:19-22).

The pattern laid out in the New Testament is still true for today. God's House is built on the foundation of the apostles and prophets. It is this foundation that establishes and empowers all the other gifts and parts of the Body to rise and become a holy dwelling place of God. This is the administration of the Ekklesia on the earth and the blueprint that will release the fullest blessing and demonstration of heaven's glory.

This is not speaking to those who simply have the titles of apostle or prophet, but those who have been called by heaven, confirmed by their fruit, and commended by the Body. It is their *function* that must be properly understood and embraced if the Church is going to mature and extend Kingdom influence to all other mountains of our culture. Instead of placing so much focus on titles and ranks, we need to pay much more attention to the grace given to these called leaders and their God-given contributions to the Body.

Unfortunately, the majority of the corporate Church in the United States has not been built on apostles and prophets, but on pastors and teachers. Though there are some valid apostolic ministries in the nation pioneering the way, most congregations do not function with an understanding of an apostolic and or prophetic foundation. Due to long-held cultural norms and a misguided belief that these gifts no longer function, many churches lack the proper foundation from which to expand and multiply.

Without apostolic ministry, churches will become ingrown and fail to extend Kingdom influence beyond themselves. Without prophetic ministry, churches will fall into programs without power and routines without purpose. Until apostles and prophets take their place in local churches, God's House will be incomplete and the Great Commission unfulfilled.

What do we look for? What are these functions? What do they provide, and how do we support their ministry in a local context? The answers to these questions will give us not only clarity concerning the needed leadership in churches, but effective prayer for those whom God is calling.

Apostolic authority within the Church provides:

- Foundational truths from Scripture to establish sound doctrine and practice.

- Long-term vision for growth and maturity of the saints.

- Insight and grace to raise up new five-fold leaders within the Body.

- Effective strategies to mobilize the people in their witness and work.

- Divine abilities to lead the Church into new territories and pioneer new initiatives.

- God-given authority to resist demonic intrusion and release heaven's blessing.

Apostles function as spiritual fathers and mothers to the household of faith. Their role is to provide vision, stability, and oversight to the Ekklesia with God-given authority and favor.

Prophetic power within the Church provides:

- Revelation concerning the person and work of the Holy Spirit in the believer's life.

- Supernatural insight concerning the spiritual realm and the activities of heaven.

- Grace to impart and activate the gifts of the Holy Spirit with power and tangible fruit.

- The call to righteousness and holiness as the standard for every believer.

- God-given foresight to enlarge the apostolic mandate on the Church.

Prophets function as visionaries and seers to complement and expand the apostolic call on the Church. Their role is to be the "eyes and ears" to the Body, interpreters of the heavenly realm so the Church will be empowered to fulfill her mission.

These two roles must function together in order to be complete. Apostles were never meant to build apart from prophetic counsel, and prophets were never meant to prophesy apart from apostolic oversight. It is the partnering of these two gifts that empower the Church to move forward with both insight and foresight.

The Foundation of the Word and Gifts of the Spirit

In practice, the predominantly Word-based churches have embraced the functions of apostolic ministry. With the values of establishing sound doctrine, preaching the gospel, and evangelizing the lost, many Evangelical denominations welcome the goals of apostolic ministry, even if they don't use the title. In like manner, predominantly Charismatic and Pentecostal churches celebrate the work of Holy Spirit and move in prophetic ministry along with the other power gifts.

This trend seems to be changing as more Evangelicals are embracing charismatic worship and more Charismatics are engaging in evangelism. Even so, I believe there is a closer collaboration needed if we are to see the fullest expression of the Kingdom displayed on the earth. Smith Wigglesworth, the famous Pentecostal evangelist, prophesied in 1947:

> "When the new church phase is on the wane, there will be evidenced in the churches something that has not been seen before: a coming together of those with an emphasis on the Word and those with an emphasis on the Spirit. When the Word and the Spirit come together, there will be the biggest movement of the Holy Spirit that the nation, and indeed the world, has ever seen."

This coming together of the Word and Spirit has been confirmed by others, including R.T. Kendall, former pastor of Westminster Chapel and Christian author:

> "By word I mean the centrality of the gospel. By spirit I mean signs, wonders and miracles. I believe that it will mean a *spontaneous combustion of power and authority* for the Church and a wake-up call to the nation."

Both nationally recognized spiritual leaders have prophesied a heaven-sent "revival" and "movement" of God, ignited by a coming together of the Word and the Spirit. If we want to embrace this word and position ourselves for heaven's "spontaneous combustion," I believe it will take the Word-based Evangelicals and the Spirit-fueled Charismatics and Pentecostals, to pursue even closer relationships in prayer, practice, and initiatives. Rather than simply acknowledging each other's presence in the room, we need to walk to the center, huddle in prayer, and start taking notes from heaven.

This next move of the Spirit will require a coming together of believers that is much deeper than in days gone by. Intercession is requiring a oneness of heart and mind that can only happen when we embrace the apostles and prophets, the Word and the Spirit, and acknowledging the value and power of each. It must influence the way we worship together and pray together, for this is the only way to access heaven's power and authority.

We Come Together, or Not at All

I saw a group of people praying in the corner, huddled together in earnest intercession. Behind them in the far distance was a mountain. I knew it represented kingdom authority and heaven's counsel. The intercessors were seeking to connect to this mountain, to align themselves in order to break through the veil and bring heaven's authority to bear on the earth. Yet, the connection was not clear. Interaction with this mountain was blocked.

Knowing we were not fully aligned, I stepped out of the group and began to move to the center, holding an invisible kind of line connected to this mountain. I knew we had to come into perfect alignment in order to break through. Finally, after continuing to move little by little toward the middle, watching this line of communication eventually settle into place, I waited.

After a few moments I saw something begin to move in the distance. Slowly but steadily I saw three distinct Beings emerge from the heart of the mountain. Closer and closer they came until I saw what they were. Three large eagles, stately, bearing immense authority and grace. As they drew closer, I knew they had been summoned. I also knew they were looking at me.

As they drew nearer a fear and dread began to come over me at the authority and might I sensed coming from them. They were deliberate, forceful, yet moving cautiously...looking... listening. At last, the three huge figures hovered immediately above me, looking down at me with a silent yet unmistakably loud message:

"We come together, or not at all."

I woke from this dream shaking in the Fear of the Lord. I had never experienced the power and presence of the Trinity before. Their call was unmistakable, and I knew it was a charge to the Church. It was the Father, Son, and Holy Spirit speaking to us as we are desperately praying for breakthrough in both the nation and in the Church.

Until we acknowledge the fullness of each person of the Godhead, we will not see the fullness of heaven come to the earth. We cannot pick and choose which expression of the Trinity we prefer. We cannot focus on one at the expense of the other. Each represents and expresses God's heart and character in a different dimension. God, our Creator and loving heavenly Father. Jesus Christ, the Word become flesh and the only way to salvation through the cross. Holy Spirit, the full expression and manifestation of the Father's heart. *They are **One**. They cannot be divided. If we want heaven to come to earth, they must come together.*

In our ongoing intercession and interaction as the Body of Christ, we must honor and celebrate those expressions and messages that are different from ours. Those who focus on the Father's unconditional love must be willing to acknowledge the call to righteousness. Those who celebrate the gifts of the Spirit must do so in love and submission to the Living Word. Those who call for a higher standard of scriptural integrity must also be willing to embrace activities of the Spirit that are not easily understood or proof-texted in Scripture.

We do not have to compromise our convictions in order to value and honor other parts of the Body and the assignment they carry (see 1 Corinthians 12:12-14). God speaks through many voices and each voice that is connected to His heart carries a needed message. Yet, each is but a part of the whole. *If we do not see the value of each part, we will miss the whole message.*

In the dream I had to get out of my comfortable corner in order to align my heart with heaven. I had to step outside my familiar group and surroundings in order to summon a response. The connection I was looking for was a heart connection. I needed to tune my heart to God's in order to comprehend the fullness of His plans and purposes. To do that, I had to be willing to go into unfamiliar territory so I could receive new input and new perspectives.

I believe the Lord is inviting us to pay more attention to the frequencies of heaven than with our own familiar wavelengths. In our prayers, our interactions, and our communications, we can honor one another and give value to the particular message each brings and the role each part plays. It is only when we hear God's purposes fully expressed through each part of the Body that we will truly connect to His heart. His Spirit within us will help to filter out the unnecessary parts and lesser things so we can hear the full counsel from heaven.

> *Just as a body, though one, has many parts, but all its many parts form one body, so it is with Christ. For we were all baptized by one Spirit so as to form one body—whether Jews or Gentiles, slave or free—and we were all given the one Spirit to drink. Even so the body is not made up of one part but of many* (1 Corinthians 12:12-14 NIV).

Bridging the Gaps

I would like to suggest several ways in which we can build bridges to better relationships with one another in our various spiritual streams. If we truly see the Kingdom vision beyond our own cultural and theological fields of influence, we will gladly reach across our fences in order to form a more perfect union.

1. Separate Dogma, Doctrine, and Opinion

Dogmas ("ordinances") are the core beliefs of the Christian faith that unite us. These include the virgin birth, the death and resurrection of Jesus Christ, the inerrancy of Scripture, the need for salvation through the cross, the returning of the Lord, etc. These are nonnegotiable for the true Christ-follower (see 1 Corinthians 15:3-5, Titus 2:11-15).

Doctrines ("teachings"), on the other hand, are interpretations of biblical practices that may vary from one fellowship to another. These would include issues like how one is baptized, involvement in the military, a woman's place in the church, speaking in tongues, eschatology, etc. These are not necessarily foundational to a person's salvation but are valid convictions to those who hold them. We can have doctrinal differences but still relate as brothers and sisters in the Body of Christ if our dogmas (core beliefs) are in place (see Acts 15:1-21).

Opinions are just that—personal preferences. These would include feelings about worship styles, the pastor's personality, the leadership structure, the programs or lack of them, the color of the walls, etc. These should never be the reason for disavowing someone or discrediting a church (see 1 Timothy 6:3-5, Philippians 1:15-18).

If we can differentiate between these three, we can more easily join together for prayer and fellowship by keeping the core values of our faith central.

> *I therefore, a prisoner for the Lord, urge you to walk in a manner worthy of the calling to which you have been called, with all humility and gentleness, with patience, bearing with one another in love, eager to maintain the unity of the Spirit in the bond of peace. There is one body and one Spirit—just as you were called to the one hope that belongs to your call—one Lord, one faith, one baptism, one God and Father of all, who is over all and through all and in all* (Ephesians 4:1-6).

2. Find Fresh Language

Every family usually has inside jokes—stories and experiences that someone outside the family just wouldn't understand. Though these can be treasured memories within the family, they can also become barriers when shared outside the family. Prophetic people tend to have their own language associated with dreams, visions, and the gifts of the Spirit such as, "The Lord told me...," "...she got slain...," "I saw in the spirit...," etc. Though easily understood by people in their camp, other sincere believers may not have those experiences or have any context for them. Mainline Evangelicals have their own expressions, as well: "I'm born again...," "...pray the sinner's prayer...," "...if it's God's will," etc. Our familiar clichés and overused phrases need to be updated so that more God-seekers can relate to what we want to share. Creative communication is sorely needed to expand our viewpoints and widen our horizons.

3. Worship in Spirit and Truth

When coming together for corporate, community-wide prayer gatherings, we can seek worship and prayer experiences that will celebrate different styles without forcing protocols. Praying in tongues may not be the best practice if another believer will be distracted by it. Reading Scripture as opposed to spontaneously prophesying can be just as meaningful if it is Spirit-inspired. Our goal must be to seek the presence of the Lord, first and foremost. We must be willing to lay down what is personally meaningful to us if it means a greater corporate encounter with God.

> *And let the peace of Christ rule in your hearts, to which indeed you were called in one body. And be thankful. Let the word of Christ dwell in you richly, teaching and admonishing one another in all wisdom, singing psalms and hymns and spiritual songs, with thankfulness in your hearts to God. And whatever you do, in word or deed, do everything in the name*

of the Lord Jesus, giving thanks to God the Father through him (Colossians 3:15-17).

4. Become "Offense-Proof"

There are countless ways in which we can be offended, both personally and corporately. Whether it's a hurtful statement made, an unfair judgment call, or a broken trust in relationship, we always have the choice to forgive and move on. Being offended may be humanly natural, but extending forgiveness and choosing to believe again is only possible by the Spirit. Let's make the decision to not let any bitter root take hold that may defile our fellowship (see Hebrews 12:15). This can happen when we choose to go quickly to those who have offended us in order to restore our fellowship. Especially when interceding for others, this principle must be enacted if our prayers are to have effect.

> *So if you are offering your gift at the altar and there remember that your brother has something against you, leave your gift there before the altar and go. First be reconciled to your brother, and then come and offer your gift* (Matthew 5:23-24).

5. Celebrate the Works of God, not Man

Our goal as the Church is to keep our eyes fixed on what the Father is doing and where the Spirit is working and moving. Our conversations should revolve around His presence and mighty acts, and not upon our individual accomplishments, exploits, and ministry advancement. Our titles, positions, and labels mean little in heaven's eyes. Our humility will be shown by taking the focus off our own ministries and building up others through edification, encouragement, and commendation. Heaven smiles on this kind of fellowship of the Spirit and will descend quickly.

Complete my joy by being of the same mind, having the same love, being in full accord and of one mind. Do nothing from selfish ambition or conceit, but in humility count others more significant than yourselves. Let each of you look not only to his own interests, but also to the interests of others (Philippians 2:2-4).

Love one another with brotherly affection. Outdo one another in showing honor (Romans 12:10).

6. Pursue the Fear of the Lord

Where some believers focus on the *mercy* of God, others focus on the *truth* of God. Where some prioritize *inclusion* for the sake of the gospel, others preach *exclusion* for the sake of righteousness. Where some side with the political "right," others side with the political "left." Contrasting values are often different sides of the same coin. There's some truth in both, yet taken to extremes, we can miss God's intended purpose and blessing as a whole. *Unless we keep the message of Christ's Kingdom and His manifest presence central to our message, we will become sidetracked and divided.*

We do this by inviting the Fear of the Lord into our midst and our fellowship. It is the Fear of the Lord that keeps our hearts in check and our views balanced by heaven's scales. If we all seek to walk in this reality, our seeming differences will be refined, purified, and sanctified for a greater purpose.

Who is the man who fears the Lord? Him will he instruct in the way that he should choose. His soul shall abide in well-being, and his offspring shall inherit the land. The friendship of the Lord is for those who fear him, and he makes known to them his covenant (Psalm 25:12-14).

Let us pray for a spontaneous combustion of apostolic authority and prophetic power in the Church. Let us learn to hold the Word of God in high esteem and celebrate the presence and work of the Holy Spirit. Let us do our part by building bridges of greater trust and deeper fellowship collaborating in meaningful demonstrations of the Kingdom. Let us celebrate the unique gifts and grace upon each part of the Body of Christ so that we can be ready to fulfill all that the Father has planned.

"This outpouring of the Holy Spirit is not only an outpouring of blessing—it is an outpouring of *authority*. God is establishing spiritual authority in the earth that He may, in this hour, bring into existence His kingdom in *power* and answer the prayers of multiplied thousands through the centuries who have interceded by crying, 'Thy kingdom come!'" —**Derek Prince**

PRAYER GUIDE

ONENESS *of* HEART AND MIND *in the* CHURCH

1. Pray that the Church would have a unified and divine jealousy over the Bride of Christ.

...Christ loved the church and gave himself up for her to make her holy, cleansing her by the washing with water through the word, and to present her to himself as a radiant church, without stain or wrinkle or any other blemish, but holy and blameless (Ephesians 5:25-27 NIV).

For no one ever hated his own flesh, but nourishes and cherishes it, just as Christ does the church, because we are members of his body (Ephesians 5:29-30).

2. Pray that believers would celebrate the Body of Christ with all its various parts, without comparisons or man-made expectations.

But as it is, God arranged the members in the body, each one of them, as he chose. If all were a single member, where would the body be? As it is, there are many parts, yet one body (1 Corinthians 12:18-20).

That there may be no division in the body, but that the members may have the same care for one another. If one member suffers, all suffer together; if one member is honored, all rejoice together. Now you are the body of Christ and individually members of it (1 Corinthians 12:25-27).

3. Pray for a corporate and collective faith that is firmly established in God's Word.

If indeed you continue in the faith, firmly established and steadfast, and not moved away from the hope of the gospel that you have heard... (Colossians 1:23).

And all these, though commended through their faith, did not receive what was promised, since God had provided something better for us, that apart from us they should not be made perfect (Hebrews 11:39-40).

4. Pray for one voice to arise from the Church that declares the good news of the Kingdom and the return of the Savior.

...Jesus went into Galilee, proclaiming the good news of God. "The time has come," he said. "The kingdom of God has come near. Repent and believe the good news!" (Mark 1:14-15 NIV)

The coming of the kingdom of God is not something that can be observed, nor will people say, "Here it is," or "There it is," because the kingdom of God is in your midst (Luke 17:20-21 NIV).

5. Pray for an increased oneness in Kingdom values and that which is eternal.

Can two walk together unless they are agreed? (Amos 3:3 NKJV)

Complete my joy by being of the same mind, having the same love, being in full accord and of one mind. Do nothing from selfish ambition or conceit, but in humility count others more significant than yourselves. Let each of you look not only to his own interests, but also to the interests of others (Philippians 2:2-4).

Live in harmony with one another. Do not be haughty but associate with the lowly. Never be wise in your own sight (Romans 12:16).

6. Pray for various streams in the Body of Christ to flow together with the same unity as the Father, Son, and Holy Spirit.

...Holy Father, keep them in Your name, which You have given me, that they may be one, even as we are one (John 17:11).

This is he who came by water and blood—Jesus Christ; not by the water only but by the water and the blood. And the Spirit is the one who testifies, because the Spirit is the truth. For there are three that testify: the Spirit and the water and the blood; and these three agree (1 John 5:6-8).

But the hour is coming, and is now here, when the true worshipers will worship the Father in spirit and truth, for the Father is seeking such people to worship him. God is spirit, and those who worship him must worship in spirit and truth (John 4:23-24).

7. Pray for the proper foundation of the apostolic and prophetic ministries to strengthen and build up the Body of Christ.

And he gave the apostles, the prophets, the evangelists, the shepherds and teachers, to equip the saints for the work of ministry, for building up the body of Christ, until we all attain to the unity of the faith and of the knowledge of the Son of God, to mature manhood, to the measure of the stature of the fullness of Christ (Ephesians 4:11-13).

The signs of a true apostle were performed among you with utmost patience, with signs and wonders and mighty works (2 Corinthians 12:12).

...I am stirring up your sincere mind by way of reminder, that you should remember the predictions of the holy prophets and the commandment of the Lord and Savior through your apostles, knowing this first of all, that scoffers will come in the last days with scoffing, following their own sinful desires (2 Peter 3:1-3).

8. **Pray for a united vision to occupy until He comes.**

    And he called his ten servants, and delivered them ten pounds, and said unto them, "Occupy till I come" (Luke 19:13 KJV).

    And they devoted themselves to the apostles' teaching and the fellowship, to the breaking of bread and the prayers (Acts 2:42).

    Behold, how good and how pleasant it is for brethren to dwell together in unity! It is like the precious ointment upon the head, that ran down upon the beard, even Aaron's beard: that went down to the skirts of his garments; as the dew of Hermon, and as the dew that descended upon the mountains of Zion: for there the Lord commanded the blessing, even life for evermore (Psalm 133:1-3 KJV).

PART II

The INTERCESSORY
COMMISSION

Chapter 7

WATCHMEN *to* THEIR POSTS

Establishing Prayer Altars

O nce we have a clear blueprint for God's government on the earth, we will be better informed in our prayers and empowered in our intercession. The call to watch and pray is core to our corporate life and witness, but must be targeted, specific, and unified. As we explore our call to prayer and what that looks like both personally and corporately, may we find greater joy in the journey and greater fruit as a result.

The Call of Watchmen

And he said to them, "My soul is very sorrowful, even to death. Remain here and watch" (Mark 14:34).

At the height of temptation and trial, Jesus told His disciples to *"watch"* with Him. As the battle was brewing in the spirit threatening to destroy Him, Jesus called upon His followers to pull away from the distractions and *"stay awake!"* They needed to look, listen, and prepare for the conflict and confrontation that was unfolding. He knew if they didn't take the necessary time to discern carefully and align their hearts and perspective with the Father's, that which was coming could ruin them.

This call to watch and pray is a constant theme throughout Scripture. In Israel, watchmen were assigned on the watchtowers of their city and given strict instructions to keep their eyes wide open and report what they saw. They were charged with warning the people of coming danger and how to prepare. Their responsibility was so great, the Lord even warned them of the consequences if they failed to report what they saw.

> *But if the watchman sees the sword coming and does not blow the trumpet, so that the people are not warned, and the sword comes and takes any one of them, that person is taken away in his iniquity, but his blood I will require at the watchman's hand* (Ezekiel 33:6).

To be a watchman meant to stay alert and scan the horizon for anything that was out of order. It required vigilance and a keen eye and ear to pick up things that others might miss. The ministry of the watchman was critical to the safety and security of a city. It was a twenty-four-hour job and mandated round-the-clock observation. However, not only was the watchman required to look and listen, he was also expected to *ask questions.*

> *I will take my stand at my watchpost and station myself on the tower, and look out* **to see what he will say to me, and what I will answer concerning my complaint** (Habakkuk 2:1).

This watchman had some complaints. Something was wrong down below and he wanted to know why. He lifted his inquiry before the Lord to receive insight and instruction on behalf of the city. This not only required the ability to shut out other voices and distractions in order to perceive things correctly, but this position was one of *interaction and conversation* with the Lord.

> *Then he who saw cried out: "Upon a watchtower I stand, O Lord, continually by day, and at my post I am stationed whole nights. And behold, here come riders, horsemen in pairs!" And he answered, "Fallen, fallen is Babylon; and all the carved images of her gods he has shattered to the ground." O my threshed and winnowed one,* **what I have heard from the Lord of hosts,** *the God of Israel,* **I announce to you** (Isaiah 21:8-10).

The call of the watchman was to inquire of the Lord and *announce* His instructions to the people. As a matter of fact, they were specifically told to *speak—continually!* Until such time that the borders were secure and the people established in safety, the Lord told them to not stop announcing His instructions.

> *On your walls, O Jerusalem, I have set watchmen; all the day and all the night* **they shall never be silent**... (Isaiah 62:6).

This is the prophetic charge today for many who have been called to be watchmen on the wall for our nation. Ours is not simply to watch and observe, but to interact with heaven and announce what we hear. It is an assignment to speak and declare what it is that the Lord of hosts is doing in the spiritual realm so that we can take our positions and respond in the natural realm. It is not enough to sit on the sidelines and worry about the attacks coming. We must take our positions and send out the warning to those who cannot see or hear what is coming. We must ask the right questions and wait for heaven's response so the call will be clear, and directives targeted. We cannot be silent until His Kingdom is secure.

Though the call of the watchman in the Old Testament was to individuals, I believe it is also a corporate call. In the New Testament, whenever

Jesus instructed His disciples to watch and pray, He spoke to them as a group (see Matthew 25:13; Mark 13:34; Luke 21:34). I believe our effectiveness as watchmen is greatly enhanced when we stand watch together. Our combined perceptions, gifts of discernment, and interpretation are expanded and enriched when we can inquire together and respond corporately to the Lord's instructions.

I believe the Lord is calling many watch groups in cities across the nation to secure our communities from spiritual attack and intrusion from enemy forces, both in the natural and the spiritual. As anti-Christ legislation increases at the community level, we need to take seriously this call to watch and pray together. We cannot stay silent any longer. We must coordinate strategically, discern correctly, and speak boldly concerning that which threatens our own borders.

Spiritual Air Supremacy

In any kind of warfare, the ability to communicate with your allies is central to any victory. Effective communication passes on vision, strategy, timing, and counsel in order to be effective in any given mission or assignment. Airwaves must be clear in order for good communication to get through. It's called "air supremacy." For intercessors, it refers to authority in the spirit, and it's this tactical strategy that can determine the battle's outcome. It's this advantage of air supremacy that our adversary wants to disrupt so that our communications are scrambled and our prayers ineffective.

I once had several dreams where the Lord highlighted the need to pray for intercessors to gain air supremacy over our territories. In the first dream, I was trying to flee from my enemy by flying up and away from the battle on the ground—flying usually represents intercession in dreams. I had often experienced this kind of dream before and always managed to fly away to safety.

However, this time, the enemy not only followed me into the air, but intercepted me and then blocked me from going any farther. He stopped directly in front of me in a distinct posture of threat. It was right before I woke up that I realized we had stopped right in front of a powerline. I knew the powerline represented my power source and connection to the heavenly realm ruled by the Spirit. I knew the Lord was warning of a "blocking" spirit that needed to be removed if my prayers were to get through and have any power.

> *...Fear not, Daniel, for from the first day that you set your heart to understand and humbled yourself before your God, your words have been heard, and I have come because of your words. The prince of the kingdom of Persia withstood me twenty-one days, but Michael, one of the chief princes, came to help me, for I was left there with the kings of Persia* (Daniel 10:12-13).

In a subsequent dream, I was on a secret mission behind enemy lines. I was being flown in and coordinating with the forces on the ground. As I landed, I was draped with a flag from World War II. In doing some research later, I found that in WWII the Allied forces won due to air supremacy! Rather than focusing on strategic bomber attacks or ground forces alone, it was the fighter pilots from above who opened the way for victory. This is a powerful picture of how ruling through prayer has strategic advantage over ground warfare, alone.

There is a strategic partnership between intercessors and those "on the ground." The intelligence we gain through our prayers must be carefully communicated to those who are on the frontlines in the various mountains of influence. It is this coordination of efforts that can assure success during times of battle and greater influence in a region. It is also important that intercessors watch for interference in communications, both in the natural and in the spiritual realms. The channels of communication in the spirit must remain open and free from any interference if we are to process strategic information and coordinate plans.

One of the common tactics of the enemy is to scramble our communications with each other and to disrupt our collaboration. This is one reason why the mountain of media is so fiercely contested. It is a major powerline of communication and information—in both realms.

We can certainly rebuke and bind the enemy's interference, but we must be careful to not get stuck in the enemy's "airspace." Some refer to this as the "second heaven" where demonic spirits operate. Though Scripture isn't definitive on this, the apostle Paul spoke of visiting the "third heaven" (see 2 Corinthians 12:2) where God rules. He was lifted up to this place to interact with heaven and gain deeper revelation from the Lord. The principle is that it is from this higher place around the throne room of God where we must deal with the adversary.

> *And you were dead in the trespasses and sins in which you once walked, following the course of this world, following the prince of the power of the air, the spirit that is now at work in the sons of disobedience...by grace you have been saved and raised **us** up with Him and seated **us** with Him in the heavenly places in Christ Jesus* (Ephesians 2:1-6).

If we get too focused on what the enemy is doing and try to fight him on his own turf—in this "second heaven"—we will be limited in our perceptions and easily distracted. This happens when we allow fear or anxiety to influence our prayers and we spend more time opposing the devil's work and rebuking him instead of declaring God's purposes and exalting the King.

Our position is to be seated with Christ, far above the demonic rulers, in order to declare God's higher rule and purpose. It is only from this posture in prayer that we have authority to clear the airwaves and remove the disruptions. Our connection to the Father as coheirs with Christ grants us the legal authority to demand submission to any lesser powers.

We also have the authority to interfere in the enemy's plans! Just as the Lord threw the enemy into confusion when Joshua was fighting for Israel (see Joshua 10:10), so the Lord can interfere in the enemy's communication lines and thwart specific assignments and attacks against us. We can declare confusion in the enemy's camp, a disconnection between opposing forces, and cut off communication lines that seek to interfere in the Lord's plans. We can speak blessing on the coordination of heaven's hosts and declare that the Chief Commander's plans and purposes will be accomplished.

> "I want to say that to you again—the King of the Kingdom of God has a government on planet earth. And the name of that government is Ecclesia, the Church, which does not need a building and does not need a service, it needs a legislative branch, a governmental branch. He has given us authority to bind, to loose, to legislate in the Heavens. We are going to take air supremacy. We are going to rule from there and we are going to drop spiritual bombs. I am going to predict to you that this will be one of the greatest facets of the next phase of the worldwide prayer movement." —**Dutch Sheets,** 2017 Aglow International Global Conference

Shifting the Atmosphere

Depending on the ruling spirit in a given territory, that spirit will affect the atmosphere. Some intercessors can tangibly feel the difference when entering cities or regions through a gift of discerning of spirits. Depending on the source and amount of spiritual activity in a given area, the atmosphere can either release heaven's favor or draw demonic resistance. The New Testament gives some examples of how the atmosphere was changed due to spiritual influence:

- A spirit of unbelief shut down an entire city from experiencing God's healing power:

  And he did not do many mighty works there, because of their unbelief (Matthew 13:58).

- A religious spirit manifested upon hearing Jesus' prophetic words and the atmosphere became filled with wrath:

  When they heard these things, all in the synagogue were filled with wrath. And they rose up and drove him [Jesus] out of the town and brought him to the brow of the hill on which their town was built, so that they could throw him down the cliff (Luke 4:28-29).

- Because of the spiritual hunger among the people gathered, healing grace became available:

  ...And the power of the Lord was with Him to heal (Luke 5:17).

- Because of the praise and worship being lifted, prison doors were supernaturally opened:

  About midnight Paul and Silas were praying and singing hymns to God, and the prisoners were listening to them, and suddenly there was a great earthquake, so that the foundations of the prison were shaken. And immediately all the

doors were opened, and everyone's bonds were unfastened
(Acts 16:25-26).

The posture of our hearts and the words from our mouths determine the atmosphere in a place. The power of our praises and our prayers can shift atmospheres in a room, a building, a neighborhood, and even an entire city. This is the amazing result of believers coming together in agreement and lifting up incense to heaven through their unified proclamations and worship. It permeates the spirit and displaces any demonic activity, making way for heaven to come down and God's presence to be made known.

> *And the whole multitude of the people were praying outside at the hour of incense. And there appeared to him an angel of the Lord standing on the right side of the altar of incense. And Zechariah was troubled when he saw him, and fear fell upon him. But the angel said to him, "Do not be afraid, Zechariah, for your prayer has been heard..."* (Luke 1:10-13).

In the early Church, the unity among believers was so strong that Scriptures speak of a "great grace" that was released in the city. This grace opened spiritual doors to miracles, signs, and wonders, along with salvations on a daily basis.

> *Now the full number of those who believed were of one heart and soul, and no one said that any of the things that belonged to him was his own, but they had everything in common. And with great power the apostles were giving their testimony to the resurrection of the Lord Jesus, and great grace was upon them all. There was not a needy person among them...* (Acts 4:32-34).

Earlier in the same chapter, it spoke of their daily fellowship and breaking of bread. Because of their corporate agreement and unified vision for the Kingdom, God's grace empowered them to do far beyond what they could have done in the natural. This should be our desire as we come together as watchmen in prayer over our cities and nation. We can pray in such agreement with heaven that the atmosphere over the city begins to be permeated with the grace and favor of the Lord.

Several years ago, our church joined with five other congregations in a 21-Day Community Fast. Our purpose was to seek the Lord together for our homes and for the city. We met every night to wait upon the Lord, worship, and confess our sins one to another. As we spent time waiting in the Lord's presence, the weight of His glory began to descend upon us and our hearts were not only broken but revived. Repentance was deep and heartfelt. Forgiveness was extended. Relationships were restored. Miracles of healing and financial breakthrough were shared. The tangible weight of God's glory was felt as we journeyed together in seeking the Lord over the course of three weeks.

The most interesting testimony we received during that time was from a local police officer who heard about our initiative. He shared that during a four-night period of this corporate fast, the police department received very few calls in the city: "We have quiet days here and there, but I can't remember the last time I worked four days—especially a nice weather weekend—and had so few calls. All the guys at work are shocked by the silent radio." During our corporate fast, the police scanners were unexpectedly quiet with almost no trouble, crime, or disturbance. Only peace. For four nights straight. We felt that this was a taste of what the Lord wanted to do on a broader scale in years to come if we would continue to make room for His presence.

> *Thus says the Lord: "Heaven is my throne, and the earth is my footstool; what is the house that you would build for me, and what is the place of my rest?"* (Isaiah 66:1)

As the corporate Church gathers in unity of heart for the purpose of glorifying Him and welcoming His presence, the spiritual climate changes and demonic influence is so diminished, it catches the attention of the community. Just imagine the doors to evangelism that could be opened if the Church created such an atmosphere of God's presence over a region. Through our prayers and worship we can silence the voice of the enemy and open the spiritual doors for the King of glory to come into our cities and draw the lost to salvation!

Establishing Prayer Altars

Not only do we need a shift in the atmosphere, we need a shift in authority—both natural and spiritual. We need God-fearing authorities in our city government and in the public square, but we must start by establishing our spiritual authority in the prayer room. The governing authority of the Ekklesia starts by establishing itself as a House of prayer.

> *...My house shall be called a house of prayer for all the nations...* (Mark 11:17).

Though it may look different from house to house, our role as a priesthood of believers is to establish a place of God's presence. In First Peter 2:9 (KJV), we are called *"...a chosen generation, a royal priesthood...."* This is part of our function as representatives of His Kingdom on the earth—to be ministers in the House of the Lord. We become witnesses to His presence and power as we minister before Him where we've been planted. However, this is not automatic.

Though we are heaven's chosen representatives in our cities, the enemy has his counterfeits seeking to take that influence and authority from us. Whichever "priesthood" is the most active in a community, will have the most authority. In Hebrews 7:12 we are told that *"...when there is a change in the priesthood, there is necessarily a change in the law as well."* In other words, *whichever priesthood is strongest in the land will rule the land.*

Ugandan pastor John Mulinde coauthored the book *Prayer Altars*[1] with American pastor Mark Daniel. Uganda experienced an amazing national transformation back in the mid-90s by practicing some of these principles. These two pastors describe the need for prayer altars to be built and established in a community in order to override the prevailing darkness. The authors state:

"There is no such thing as neutral spiritual ground. Either there will be a predominance of holy altars drawing the presence of God or unholy altars drawing the powers of darkness...the altar that is most active will control the territory and will influence everything in that territory."

This is a needed wake-up call to realize that if the Church doesn't establish its spiritual authority in prayer, the door will be open for the enemy to come in and devour the land by default. Numerous times in the Old Testament, God told His people to build altars and make a sacrifice to the Lord. This practice continues in the New Testament as we give sacrifices of praise and thanksgiving at the altar of worship (see Hebrews 13:15).

What are prayer altars? A prayer altar is a *sacred time* and *sacred place* where one meets with God. It is a place where God's presence is the priority, over and above our list of personal needs or corporate agendas. It starts with inviting His presence and waiting upon Him as we read His Word, worship, and follow the leading of the Holy Spirit in changing the spiritual climate over our regions. We don't pray *for* His presence, but *from* it.

How do prayer altars function in the city? Altars are gateways to the spiritual realm and can be established anywhere that someone draws the attention of spiritual forces—good or bad. Abortion clinics, prostitution hubs, corrupt establishments, New Age businesses, churches that are cults, etc. All these become forms of unholy altars that draw the presence of evil into a community. Until the priesthood of believers establishes *holy altars* to counter these ungodly gateways, the darkness will prevail due to the number of unholy altars built and maintained.

> "When the altar of the Lord is not being maintained or is in disrepair—not functioning properly or even not functioning at all—altars of darkness start to come into the land to fill the void...The only way to turn things back around is for someone in the land to rebuild the altar of the Lord." —John Mulinde[2]

This means consistent maintenance of a prayer altar through people who give themselves to prayer, worship, repentance, covenant relationship, and walking in holiness as unto the Lord. This is not just another prayer meeting, but an intentional drawing of God's tangible presence to displace the dark forces at work. This cannot happen through special services, conferences, or one-time events. To change the atmosphere over a community, it cannot happen in one congregation or under one leader. If that would work, we would have seen changes by now!

This is a *lifestyle* of building and maintaining prayer altars of His presence throughout the city and throughout the week, both personally and corporately. Whether it's small home groups, prayer ministries, or an intentional time of prayer in community gatherings, God is looking to establish a place of His presence in homes, churches, cities, and regions on a consistent basis. This means pursuing God, not as some spiritual discipline, but with a deep-felt heart cry, pressing in through worship and prayer *until* His presence overshadows us.

For those who are not accustomed to this kind of focused and inti-mate prayer, it can start by incorporating times of intercession in a weekly service. If congregations are to be houses of prayer as Jesus commanded, pastors can nurture this value during corporate services in various ways: take time during the service to pray for specific needs in the commu-nity, pray for one another at the altar, invite intercessors to lead out at appointed times, pray for other churches in the city, corporately recite prayers from Scripture, etc.

Intercessory groups can be encouraged to pray before services and congregants can be invited to submit prayer requests for further prayer during the week. Until we establish prayer as a core value of our faith, we will not mature into the deeper things of God, nor position ourselves to encounter His presence.

When I speak of God's presence, I'm not talking about His *omni-presence,* which is evident in creation (see Romans 1:20). I'm not talking about His *indwelling* presence which we receive upon salvation (see Ephesians 3:16-17). I'm talking about the *manifest* presence of God that comes *upon* us to demonstrate to the world, the glory and goodness of the Father (see Acts 1:8). Where the indwelling Spirit is for us and our own edification, God's manifest presence is for others. It is when the manifest presence of the Lord comes that there are signs and wonders (see Acts 4:30), healings, salvations, and deliverance. It is in the tangible presence of God that we go beyond believing and start experiencing the goodness and greatness of God. It is a demonstration of the Kingdom and the com-mon practice in the early Church to bring the lost to salvation.

Unless believers establish and maintain prayer altars unto the Lord throughout their city, the adversary will continue to establish unholy altars that draw the forces of darkness. These altars of humanism, pagan-ism, cultism, and other counterfeit practices attract the enemy and block the flow of God's presence. We must pray for a divine strategy to stir us to action and inspire other believers in our churches and community in establishing these prayer altars. May our hearts burn with a passion to keep the fires going on the altars of prayer and worship to make room for God's presence to descend upon our cities.

Endnotes

1. John Mulinde and Mark Daniel, *Prayer Altars: A Strategy that Is Changing Nations* (Kampala, Uganda: World Trumpet Mission, 2013).

2. Ibid.

PRAYER GUIDE

ESTABLISHING
PRAYER *in the* CITY

1. Pray for a greater spiritual hunger among all believers to know the presence of God through the power of the Holy Spirit.

Whom have I in heaven but you? And there is nothing on earth that I desire besides you (Psalm 73:25).

...If anyone thirsts, let him come to me and drink. Whoever believes in me, as the Scripture has said, "Out of his heart will flow rivers of living water." Now this he said about the Spirit, whom those who believed in him were to receive... (John 7:37-39).

2. Pray for a collective vision for the city to be blanketed in prayer.

All these with one accord were devoting themselves to prayer... (Acts 1:14).

And they devoted themselves to the apostles' teaching and the fellowship, to the breaking of bread and the prayers (Acts 2:42).

And the Lord said to Paul one night in a vision, "Do not be afraid, but go on speaking and do not be silent, for I am with you, and no one will attack you to harm you, for I have many in this city who are my people" (Acts 18:9-10).

3. Ask the for Lord to raise up watchmen called of the Lord.

On your walls, O Jerusalem, I have set watchmen; all the day and all the night they shall never be silent. You who put the Lord in remembrance, take no rest, and give him no rest until he establishes Jerusalem and makes it a praise in the earth (Isaiah 62:6-7).

I wait for the Lord, my soul waits, and in His word I do hope. My soul waits for the Lord more than those who watch for the morning—yes, more than those who watch for the morning (Psalm 130:5-6 NKJV).

4. Pray for pastors and church leaders to be gripped with the urgency of prayer.

In the path of your judgments, O Lord, we wait for you; your name and remembrance are the desire of our soul. My soul yearns for you in the night; my spirit within me earnestly seeks you... (Isaiah 26:8-9).

I rise before dawn and cry for help; I hope in your words. My eyes are awake before the watches of the night, that I may meditate on your promise (Psalm 119:147-148).

5. Ask the Lord for tangible results to prayer that would strengthen and encourage corporate faith.

When Peter came to himself, he said, "Now I am sure that the Lord has sent His angel and rescued me from the hand of Herod and from all that the Jewish people were expecting." When he realized this, he went to the house of Mary, the mother of John whose other name was Mark, where many were gathered together and were praying (Acts 12:11-12).

...On him we have set our hope that he will deliver us again. You also must help us by prayer, so that many will give thanks on our behalf for the blessing granted us through the prayers of many (2 Corinthians 1:10-11).

6. Pray for those called to build prayer altars throughout the city. Pray that every sphere of the culture would be covered in prayer.

So in the lowest parts of the space behind the wall, in open places, I stationed the people by their clans, with their swords, their spears, and their bows. And I looked and arose and said to the nobles and to the officials and to the rest of the people, "Do not be afraid of them. Remember the Lord, who is great and awesome, and fight for your brothers, your sons, your daughters, your wives, and your homes" (Nehemiah 4:13-14).

And every day Mordecai walked in front of the court of the harem to learn how Esther was and what was happening to her (Esther 2:11).

And when they had entered, they went up to the upper room, where they were staying.... All these with one accord were devoting themselves to prayer, together with the women and Mary the mother of Jesus, and his brothers (Acts 1:13-14).

7. **Pray that the Lord would stir unbelievers to ask for prayer.**

Inquire of the Lord for us, for Nebuchadnezzar king of Babylon is making war against us. Perhaps the Lord will deal with us according to all his wonderful deeds and will make him withdraw from us (Jeremiah 21:2).

King Zedekiah sent...to Jeremiah the prophet, saying, "Please pray for us to the Lord our God" (Jeremiah 37:3).

8. **Pray for God's tangible presence to come in the midst of His people to bring comfort, rest, strength, and greater empowering from the Spirit.**

The Lord replied [to the nation of Israel], *"My Presence will go with you, and I will give you rest"* (Exodus 33:14 NIV).

Surely you have granted him unending blessings and made him glad with the joy of your presence. For the king trusts in the Lord; through the unfailing love of the Most High he will not be shaken (Psalm 21:6-7 NIV).

And suddenly there came from heaven a sound like a mighty rushing wind, and it filled the entire house where they were sitting. And divided tongues as of fire appeared to them and rested on each one of them. And they were all filled with the Holy Spirit and began to speak in other tongues as the Spirit gave them utterance (Acts 2:2-4).

Chapter 8

Moving from SWORD *to* SCEPTER

From Warriors to Rulers

It was during my morning prayer time in early 2018 when I heard in my spirit, "It is time to move from the *sword* to the *scepter.*" It seemed to come out of nowhere. Yet, I had been considering the ongoing spiritual battles we are facing as a nation, wondering why we weren't seeing more breakthrough. I could sense a weariness among many who have been interceding for decades and wondered if our strategy was still applicable. We'd been taught to be warriors in the spiritual battle, wielding our swords against the attacks of the enemy. I knew many intercessors who constantly felt under attack when they engaged in spiritual warfare. I sensed there was more to the plan than simply fighting on the battlefield with no end in sight.

I knew the Lord was answering my quandary. Through more prayer and reflection, I had a growing realization that the Lord was announcing a new strategy in dealing with the demonic forces coming against the Church. Where I had been spending all my time on the battlefield with sword in hand, the Lord was now directing me to another place, with another weapon. He was calling me up higher—to the throne room. I was being called to the throne room; and instead of using my sword, He was extending me His scepter as a new weapon against the enemy.

I could picture myself walking off the battlefield, tired and exhausted from yet another spiritual skirmish with sword in hand. Knowing there were more attacks coming, I joyfully looked to the castle on the hill and began to ascend in answer to the King's invitation. I finally realized I wasn't expected to stay on the battlefield to face the enemy over and over again. My Father had something much better in mind.

I am an heir, after all. My Father is King and I have been created to reign with Him. The scepter was being extended to me and I had not considered its potential. I had been so focused on being effective in battle, I forgot that I was not created as a warrior, but as an heir with Christ, destined to rule and reign in my Father's Kingdom.

> *Yet you have made him a little lower than the heavenly beings and crowned him with glory and honor. You have given him dominion over the works of your hands; you have put all things under his feet* (Psalm 8:5-6).

As this mental picture unfolded in my mind, it struck my spirit with anticipation and a great sense of expectation. One of my strongest motivational gifts is that of a "ruler" (see Romans 12:6-8 KJV). Given my specific mandate from the Lord as a five-fold prophetic voice to the Church, I've always felt that the gifts God has given me are symbolic of what He has given the Church. Even as I saw myself ascending that hill, I saw the Body of Christ ascending with me. I knew God was calling *us* up higher to this place of ruling with Him, scepter in hand.

This call is not only about the weapons we are using, it is about our posture of hearts and the purpose of our warfare. It is about the vision we carry when we intercede and the larger blueprint of the Kingdom. *It is learning to discern when to war and when to rule; when to use the sword, and when to use the scepter.* I now believe the Lord is transitioning the prayer movement to rule from the throne room and not spend as much time on the battlefield. I believe we are being repositioned as rulers instead of warriors and being reminded of our eternal destiny as Kingdom heirs.

In terms of practical intercession, this will require a shift in our thinking. It will require a shift in the attitude of our prayers. It will be a shift in our identities as we secure our inheritance, not because we have *fought* for it or *earned* it as a warrior, but because He has *given it to us as coheirs with Christ* (see Colossians 1:12). Rather than establishing His Kingdom on the earth from the battlefield with sword in hand, we will be rendering decisions with His scepter, thus securing our inheritance and establishing the throne.

The Purpose of the Sword

If we are to make this transition, we must learn about the purpose of the sword and the purpose of the scepter. We must understand when to use each and how this will affect our prayers. In the Old Testament, the sword was used in times of war (see Job 5:20). Numerous examples are given of how the sword was used for specific purposes when God's people were facing an attack from their enemy.

The sword was used to execute justice:

And I will bring a sword upon you, that shall execute vengeance for the covenant... (Leviticus 26:25).

For I lift up my hand to heaven and swear, as I live forever, if I sharpen my flashing sword and my hand takes hold on judgment, I will take vengeance on my adversaries and will repay those who hate me (Deuteronomy 32:40-41).

...be afraid of the sword, for wrath brings the punishment of the sword, that you may know there is a judgment (Job 19:28-29).

The sword was used to displace an enemy:

...This is no other than the sword of Gideon the son of Joash, a man of Israel; God has given into his hand Midian and all the camp (Judges 7:14).

You shall chase your enemies, and they shall fall before you by the sword (Leviticus 26:7).

In the Old Testament the sword represented strength and power in battle. It was used when under attack or when trying to gain new territory.

In the New Testament, the sword is mentioned several times, each with a slightly different purpose.

Jesus brought a sword, not to destroy, but to divide and separate:

Do not think that I have come to bring peace to the earth. I have not come to bring peace, but a sword. For I have come to set a man against his father, and a daughter against her mother, and a daughter-in-law against her mother-in-law. And a person's enemies will be those of his own household (Matthew 10:34-36).

Jesus was saying the sword was going to divide and separate those who were true to His household and those who weren't. The message of the

Kingdom would be so divisive, even families would be separated by the cutting edge of His words.

The sword is used as a discerning tool and means to purify our hearts:

For the word of God is living and active, sharper than any two-edged sword, piercing to the division of soul and of spirit, of joints and of marrow, and discerning the thoughts and intentions of the heart (Hebrews 4:12).

Here again, the sword is used as a tool to separate the good from the bad, the true from the false. It is sharp because it gets to the point! It is a penetrating tool to get to the truth.

The sword is a tool for intercession:

And take the helmet of salvation, and the sword of the Spirit, which is the word of God, praying at all times in the Spirit, with all prayer and supplication... (Ephesians 6:17-18).

Our most powerful intercession happens when we declare God's Word over situations. When rightly applied, His Word is just like a sword that cuts through lies and deception and clears the way for God's answers to get through.

The sword is alluded to as a weapon of righteousness:

By truthful speech, and the power of God; with the weapons of righteousness for the right hand and for the left (2 Corinthians 6:7).

Our righteousness acts like a sword in prayer. Our speech becomes powerful as we declare the righteousness of God from a pure heart.

The sword was given to governing authorities in order to punish evil:

> *For he is God's servant for your good. But if you do wrong, be afraid, for he does not bear the sword in vain. For he is the servant of God, an avenger who carries out God's wrath on the wrongdoer* (Romans 13:4).

Just as the sword was used in the Old Testament to execute justice or vengeance, so God has given governing authorities on this side of the cross the right to release His wrath on the wrongdoer with a "sword," a tool of judicial punishment. It even causes a healthy Fear of the Lord to fall on the land to dissuade evil.

Thus, the sword in both testaments refers to a means of God's power to both destroy His enemies as well as represent His truth. As we look at the meaning of the scepter and its use, we will find that *where the sword may represent **power**, the scepter represents **authority**.*

The Purpose of the Scepter

The term "scepter" is only found in the Old Testament and was generally understood to be a type of rod or staff. When used as *hâqaq*, it means to decree, govern, or make into law. When used as *šêbet*, it is in reference to ruling a clan or tribe. The scepter was always associated with governing authority (see Ezekiel 19:14). In the New Testament, the word used for "scepter" is *rhabdos* and means rod or staff. It indicates a cane or a baton of royalty; and when applied to kings, it indicated the severest and most rigorous rule.

> *From his mouth comes a sharp sword with which to strike down the nations, and he will rule them with a rod of iron. He will tread the winepress of the fury of the wrath of God the Almighty* (Revelation 19:15).

The purpose of the scepter is very different from the sword. The examples provided should give some keen insight as to how the scepter might be used in intercession and how we might discern which weapon to utilize when faced with a threat from the enemy.

The scepter was given to heirs:

> *Then Israel sang this song: "Spring up, O well!—Sing to it!—the well that the princes made, that the nobles of the people dug, with the scepter and with their staffs..."* (Numbers 21:17-18).

Any warrior can use a sword, but you must be an heir to use a scepter. When holding the scepter, you automatically have the same authority as your Father. It's *just as if* He were the one rendering the decisions and judgments.

The scepter was used to take dominion:

> *...and a scepter shall rise out of Israel; it shall crush the forehead of Moab and break down all the sons of Sheth. Edom shall be dispossessed; Seir also, his enemies, shall be dispossessed. Israel is doing valiantly. And one from Jacob*

shall exercise dominion and destroy the survivors of cities!
(Numbers 24:17-19)

*As the mountains surround Jerusalem, so the Lord surrounds
his people, from this time forth and forevermore. For the scepter of wickedness shall not rest on the land allotted to the righteous...* (Psalm 125:2-3).

When the scepter is in hand, it guarantees dominion and authority
over any illegal intruder. Unlike a sword that is wielded in order to activate its power, a scepter is simply held with authority granted to the one
holding it. God will not allow a substitute ruler or counterfeit heir to rob
us of our inheritance when His scepter rules.

The scepter provides protection and safety:

*Even though I walk through the valley of the shadow of death,
I will fear no evil, for you are with me; your rod* [scepter] *and
your staff, they comfort me* (Psalm 23:4).

Shepherd your people with your staff [scepter], *the flock of
your inheritance, who dwell alone in a forest in the midst of
a garden land...The nations shall see and be ashamed of all
their might...they shall come trembling out of their strongholds; they shall turn in dread to the Lord our God, and they
shall be in fear of you* (Micah 7:14-17).

The scepter not only symbolizes great authority, but strong security
against any evil. When we have the scepter in hand, it brings us assurance
of the protection afforded to us by the King's heavenly guard. This protection is so strong, it causes even our enemies to take notice and fear the
authority we have.

The scepter establishes God's covenant with His people:

"...The pride of Assyria shall be laid low, and the scepter of Egypt shall depart. I will make them strong in the Lord, and they shall walk in his name," declares the Lord (Zechariah 10:11-12).

The scepter signifies an everlasting covenant with Yahweh, our God, and our right to inherit everything He promised. We carry His name when we carry His scepter and our legacy is secure by virtue of its sovereign authority.

The scepter deals with rebellion:

Testing will surely come. And what if even the scepter, which the sword despises, does not continue? declares the Sovereign Lord (Ezekiel 21:13 NIV).

The scepter shall not depart from Judah, nor the ruler's staff from between his feet, until tribute comes to him; and to him shall be the obedience of the peoples (Genesis 49:10).

When the spirit of rebellion is at work, it is the scepter that has the authority to render it null and void. Those who want to rebel against the King with the sword hate the scepter because of what it represents. It signifies absolute rule whereby every other power and principality must bow.

The scepter grants favor:

And when the king saw Queen Esther standing in the court, she won favor in his sight, and he held out to Esther the

*golden scepter that was in his hand. Then Esther approached
and touched the tip of the scepter. And the king said to her,
"What is it, Queen Esther? What is your request? It shall be
given you, even to the half of my kingdom"* (Esther 5:2-3).

Because of her relationship with the king, Esther was given great favor when the scepter was extended to her. Not only was she granted entrance before the king, she was guaranteed a response even before she uttered her request. Think of the ramifications in prayer! When we establish an intimate history with the King, He will extend His scepter to us and grant us our requests before we even speak. In this context, the scepter is an extension of His great mercy and kindness and is a powerful tool in prayer when extending God's goodness to those who are earnestly seeking Him.

The scepter authorizes Kingdom legislation:

*Gilead is mine; Manasseh is mine; Ephraim is my helmet;
Judah is my scepter* ["law giver"] (Psalm 60:7).

*Your throne, O God, will last for ever and ever; a scepter of
justice will be the scepter of your kingdom* (Psalm 45:6 NIV).

Unlike the sword, the scepter authorizes us to legislate the King's decrees and orders. Where we can use the sword to *declare*, to make known or clear, what the King *has already spoken*, it is with the scepter that we can *decree or establish a new thing*, by order of the King. It is from the throne room that decrees are made. Rulers are the ones who make these new edicts. Warriors, on the other hand, declare the orders that have already been given, as they are defending His reign. When we understand the authority behind the scepter, we will no longer see it as just another power tool! It represents identity, security, and a lasting legacy for those who know how to use it.

Using the SWORD may destroy your enemies, but using the SCEPTER will secure your inheritance!

...“Come, let us go up to the mountain of the Lord, to the house of the God of Jacob, that he may teach us his ways and that we may walk in his paths.” For out of Zion shall go the law, and the word of the Lord from Jerusalem. He shall judge between the nations and shall decide disputes for many peoples; and they shall beat their swords into plowshares, and their spears into pruning hooks; nation shall not lift up sword against nation, neither shall they learn war anymore (Isaiah 2:3-4).

Positioned as a Ruler in Prayer

Both the sword and the scepter release God’s power and authority because they are instruments of His will and His Word. The difference, however, depends on the specific purpose they are being used for *and the posture of the one using it. Spiritual warfare is not as much about the strength or performance of the warrior as it is about the supremacy and authority of the King.* Kings have nothing to prove. Rulers do not strive to be known. Our attitude in prayer should reflect Christ’s attitude when He humbled Himself and took on the nature of a servant, yet functioned as a king (see Philippians 2:5-11).

In prayer, intercessors can tend to focus too much on the battle and what the enemy is doing. Much time and energy can be expended in calling down the adversary rather than simply stating the King’s decrees. We must avoid the temptation to believe the volume of our prayers, the passion of our cries, or the force of our delivery will somehow defeat the devil. This is like waving around a flashy sword in hopes that someone sees it!

If we believe our victory is secured because of our own merits as a warrior, our identity and call is misplaced. Our spiritual adversary is determined to wear out many intercessors through needless battles unless we change our strategy. **We must begin to defeat the enemy through executing righteous judgments from the throne room instead of fighting with him on the battlefield.**

Jesus gave us some great examples. When a storm, driven by a demonic principality, tore over the lake where Jesus and the disciples were, Jesus stood in the boat and simply spoke three words, *"Peace! Be still!"* There was no battle. There was no contest. Only a word (see Mark 4:39-40). The words He spoke certainly cut like a sword, but they came from the posture of a ruler.

When His disciples wanted to use the sword at His arrest, Jesus said, *"Put your sword back into its place. For all who take the sword will perish by the sword"* (Matthew 26:52). Jesus knew the bigger picture concerning the battle before Him and He took the posture of a king. When confronted by Pilate soon after His arrest, Jesus responded to Pilate's question about His kingship by stating:

> *My kingdom is not of this world. If my kingdom were of this world, my servants would have been fighting, that I might not be delivered over to the Jews. But my kingdom is not from the world."* Then Pilate said to him, "So you are a king?" Jesus answered, "You say that I am a king. For this purpose I was born and for this purpose I have come into the world..."* (John 18:36-37).

Jesus knew that man was no match for His sovereign reign. Knowing He could have called on His disciples and the heavenly hosts to fight on His behalf, He laid aside the sword and walked in the anointing of the King. Where the enemy wanted to engage Him in battle, He simply stood in His authority; and as a result, won the war. This strategy was followed many times by His followers after He ascended to heaven. When threatened or attacked, the disciples continually stood in their God-given authority and ruled in the midst of their enemies through prayer, praise, and the proclamation of the Kingdom of God.

There is one other aspect in our spiritual warfare that must be acknowledged. There will be times when our authority in the battle will be seemingly questioned or blocked. If neither the sword nor the scepter is working, it may be because the accuser has a legal hold over us that must be dealt with in the courtrooms of heaven. This will require us to wait on the Lord for any needed repentance, forgiveness, or cutting away of our past in order to clear our name and restore our authority. Once any charges against us are dropped and the case closed by the Righteous Judge, we are then free to pick up the scepter and rule once again.

Ultimately, there will be a time when the battles cease, and the courtroom is closed. It is the throne room, alone, that is eternal. All that happens in those two positions are for the sole purpose of getting us to the throne room. It is in the throne room where we stand as joint heirs, not as warriors or defendants. It is there in His glory we stand as sons and daughters who hold the scepter of Kingdom authority and rule.

I would propose the best place to start in prayer is in the throne room. Assume that position from the very beginning and don't even think of going on the battlefield unless it's absolutely necessary. If we are to be seated with Him in heavenly places, the throne room is the place to be. It's from this vantage point that we can see much farther than we can when stuck in ground warfare.

The following Prayer Guide can help establish some new attitudes and mindsets as you posture yourself as a ruler in prayer. Regardless of the issues you are facing or the battles at hand, begin to picture yourself in the throne room, arrayed in royal robes, standing as an heir of the King.

Whether you declare the Word of God or spontaneously prophesy God's heart and purpose, know that your confidence in who and whose you are can produce a shift in the atmosphere and tip the scales in heaven's favor.

PRAYER GUIDE

SECURING OUR INHERITANCE *with* *the* SCEPTER

Know that our spiritual authority in prayer comes more from *who we are* than from *what we pray*.

Remember who and whose you are before you even pray. It is not the words you speak that are the most powerful, but the condition of your heart and your faithfulness in following His lead. Your intercession should be an overflow of your heart's focus on Him, not a check-off list of prayer needs.

1. Envision yourself seated with Christ on the throne and lean into His heart. Ask Him to cleanse your eyes and ear gates in order to accurately receive from His Spirit. Focus on His immense love, His absolute sovereignty, and His miraculous power at work—in you!

2. Determine to be clear of any encumbrance, personal agenda, or self-centered thoughts. Release any negative attitudes or judgments and invite the Lord to renew your mind according to His Word.

3. Remember the power of your heart attitudes, even more than the words you speak. Invite the Holy Spirit to reveal new things in new ways. See yourself as a coheir with Christ, one called to rule and speak for the King.

Focus your prayers on declaring His purposes rather than on fixing the problems.

Rather than rehashing the problem—as if He doesn't know it—or suggesting ways for Him to fix the problem, declare His Word and let His decrees stand on their own merit. Don't allow the circumstances or your emotions dictate the outcome. Seek His heart through His Word and speak His purposes into existence.

1. Start in praise and worship, declaring His lordship over your life and situations.

2. As you lift various issues before the Lord, thank Him for His coming answers and His superior ability to accomplish His purposes.

3. Replace any fear or anxiety with faith in the One who knows the perfect solution and means to break through any barrier.

4. Declare various Scriptures over people, situations, and issues and prophesy the victory of the Lord.

Focus your prayers on God's increasing Kingdom instead of the world's crumbling systems.

Remember that the government and all that pertains to our well-being is on Christ's shoulders, not ours. It is His Kingdom that is ever-increasing, regardless of what the headlines say. Instead of praying "against" things, pray "for" His rule to be established, His people to come into alignment, and His purposes to stand.

1. As each issue or individual is lifted up, declare God's redemptive purposes, changing any negative parts into tools in the Lord's hands.

2. Whatever destructive pattern is at work, flip it around to declare God's intentions. Speak the opposite of what the enemy is seeking to accomplish.

3. Prophesy the increase of God's government over individuals and situations to displace the enemy's lies and schemes.

Address the *sin issues*—rotting carcasses on the land—instead of *fighting the devil*—shooting the circling vultures.

If we do our part in clearing our hearts and coming clean before the Lord, the enemy will have no ground from which to take hold. A good ruler will acknowledge where he or she has gone wrong and make things right. We will attract heavenly hosts to war on our behalf when our hearts are clear and any charges brought against us have been canceled.

1. Repent of any known sin or cause for enemy interference and ask forgiveness for those who do not yet know the truth.

2. Ask for further revelation concerning any roadblock or hindrance to the Spirit's work.

3. Apply the blood of Jesus where necessary and celebrate the victory of the cross.

4. Declare every path free of obstruction and every divine connection free from interference.

Shift from a warfare mentality to a Presence reality.

When we spend time in the King's presence, we are changed. Our faith is secured, our strength is revived, and our vision clarified. Throughout biblical history, the greatest victories came because of God's tangible presence in the battle, not because of man's skill at warfare—the battle of Jericho in Joshua 6; Jehoshaphat's army in Second Chronicles 20; the cloud of His presence at the Red Sea.

1. Spend time reflecting on the Lord's presence, becoming more aware of His tangible weight in the room.

2. Picture yourself at His throne with scepter in hand, listening to His voice for further instructions and understanding.

3. Invite His presence to hover over various people He brings to mind so that the atmosphere would be shifted and His glory known in very personal ways.

4. Lift high the praises of God to displace the works of darkness, demonstrating the overarching authority of heaven that has already defeated hell and its minions.

...how much more will those who receive God's abundant provision of grace and of the gift of righteousness reign in life through the one man, Jesus Christ! (Romans 5:17 NIV)

Chapter 9

WARFARE *That* WORKS

Practices from the Early Church

Confronting the Ring of Power

I met Cynthia Dunbar several years ago, through a mutual friend, as the Republican National Committeewoman for Virginia. She is also a lawyer and educational advocate, as well as a Spirit-filled believer and intercessor. We instantly connected and started sharing our common concerns about the government and how we were praying concerning national issues. With her involvement in politics, including a run for a seat in Virginia's Congress, her inside perspective was very revealing. In an interview with Intercessors for America, she described the reality of the spiritual warfare taking place in the governmental realm and the seduction of power that immediately faces anyone who enters politics:

> "There's such a desire for power, that even well-intentioned, good people become so consumed for power and name-recognition that they become Machiavellian [deceitful, unscrupulous], and the end justifies the means.

I've seen it take even good men and good women...it's kind of like the *Lord of the Rings*, once you put that ring of power on, it does something to you. The only way you can be immune to it is if you are truly being motivated by pursuing God, because God is the Highest Authority."
—Cynthia Dunbar

Another trusted high-level intercessory prayer leader, who has been stationed in Washington, DC for more than twenty-five years, made a similar comment. I asked her what piece of advice she would give to the many intercessors who come to DC to pray on-site. She said it's very easy to get caught up in the atmosphere that is charged with immense power. If intercessors don't guard their hearts through humility, the ruling principalities of power and greed begin to influence the way they pray in their attitudes and posture.

These testimonies describe the seduction of supernatural powers at work when we are unaware of their presence and activity. The ruling principalities and territorial spirits that hover over a city or region can influence everyone, Christians included. Corporate strongholds on the land open spiritual gateways for the enemy to come in and rule. Depending on what people in that city are collectively reaching for, preoccupied with, and pursuing, either heaven's hosts will be drawn in or the hordes of darkness will come.

The rise of the occult in the entertainment industry and in community halls is now frighteningly real. Witchcraft is no longer simply a nemesis in children's fairy tales or some backroom fetish for a few. Witches and warlocks now openly ply their trade on city streets and over social media. Worse yet, some are even claiming to be Christians and benefiting from the white magic the craft claims. Casting spells are now available online and the popularity of Harry Potter has made the study of witchcraft seem innocent and childlike. We are being fooled and fueled by a dark force whose only desire is to steal, kill, and destroy this next generation before ever tasting of the authentic realities of heaven's supernatural Kingdom.

The spirit of rebellion in the land has opened a wide door for witchcraft to enter. *"For rebellion is as the sin of witchcraft, and stubbornness is as iniquity and idolatry..."* (1 Samuel 15:23 NKJV). This hasn't just come from nonbelievers. Even the Church has played into the enemy's hands. Because of our struggle to embrace and submit to spiritual authority, we have allowed rebellion in our ranks, opening a door to counterfeit authority and demonic deception.

Our lack of corporate agreement and unwillingness to commit to one another in a covenant community also benefits the enemy's playbook. Where witches join covens in order to form their circles of power, believers avoid belonging to any church for fear of being controlled. As a result, we are left without protection, void of unity, and open prey for the dark side. If only believers understood the power of covenant as much as witches do.

If we are to effectively confront and deal with these dark alliances crashing in on us, we must update our information and upgrade our tools. The weapons of our warfare are bordering on being carnal if we keep doing things the same way without seeing any lasting change. We need to revisit some terminology and understanding of what "spiritual warfare" truly is—and isn't.

Principalities and Territorial Spirits

For we do not wrestle against flesh and blood, but against principalities, against powers, against the rulers of the darkness of this age, against spiritual hosts of wickedness in the heavenly places. Therefore, take up the whole armor of God, that you may be able to withstand in the evil day, and having done all, to stand (Ephesians 6:12-13 NKJV).

The list of spiritual forces seems to indicate a progression—a ranking of sorts. Just as there is an army of heavenly hosts with ranks and assignments, so is there a demonic force of legions. They are organized and given assignments over people, cities, regions, and nations (see Daniel 10:13). They only have power when we give it to them. It is through our agreement with their purpose—knowingly or unknowingly—that gives them a legal right to operate in our spheres of influence.

Personally, I've been set free from demonic oppression several times in my life and have ministered in deliverance through the years to many leaders. In each case, the pattern is the same. There is an ungodly belief that gets formed in the mind and, left unchecked, it forms a stronghold. If that stronghold is acted on repeatedly, it creates legal ground for demonic intrusion. Until that ungodly belief is discovered and converted to a godly belief, freedom cannot come and will not last.

If you understand the principles of personal deliverance, the same principles apply to corporate deliverance. This is helpful when discerning and dealing with principalities and territorial spirits. When enough people in a geographic area think on, create, or agree with an ungodly belief system of any kind—addiction, pornography, trafficking, rebellion, greed, etc.—it will become a corporate mindset and stronghold. The collective ungodly belief opens a door to the enemy, and territorial spirits now have legal access over that area. Whereas an individual can be demonically oppressed and harassed because of a personal ungodly belief, so can an entire group of people come under a corporate stronghold because of their collective ungodly beliefs. This is a critical component in understanding what must happen to be free of them!

"Principalities" are ruling spirits (*arche*), meaning *first*, because they are the "principal" spirits operating somewhere. In the angel Gabriel's exchange with Daniel, he said that the *"Prince of the kingdom of Persia"* resisted him, implying it was a spiritual *princ*ipality over Persia. "Territorial spirits" are not specifically mentioned in Scriptures, but there are some references that allude to the type of spirits they are and how they function, as in Daniel.

In Mark 5:9, Jesus addressed a man demonized by a spirit called "Legion." This demonic spirit begged Jesus to not send him "out of the country," implying it would lose its authority if it left the geographic area. A territorial spirit simply refers to this kind of demonic spirit that is influencing a specific territory because of a corporate stronghold in place. It has gained authority in *that* territory. As we will see later in this chapter, the only way to properly deal with corporate strongholds is through corporate deliverance and a changing of those ungodly beliefs collectively. Even so, we as individual believers are greatly affected by these corporate ruling spirits.

The previously stated Scripture from Ephesians on spiritual warfare is often misunderstood. Rather than saying that we are the ones to take on these dark forces, it simply states that our battles are a *result* of their activity. The challenges, struggles, and seeming attacks we experience are often but a reflection of a bigger battle taking place in the heavenly realms. We are wrestling with them indirectly because of their influence in the spirit realm. "Therefore," we are to wear our *protective* armor of the Lord and stand. Not engage with the dark forces, but stand. Later in Ephesians 6:17, the sword is mentioned as a weapon in prayer; declaring God's will over our lives in order to stay standing.

A common practice in spiritual warfare is to rebuke the devil in these high places of authority. However, all the instances of rebuking a demonic spirit in Scripture are when ministering to people on the ground. Jesus rebuked sickness, disease, and evil spirits that were operating in people throughout His ministry (see Mark 1:25, 9:25). We have this authority because He gave it to us (see Luke 10:19). There is no instance of rebuking principalities or territorial spirits.

John Paul Jackson, a nationally recognized and well-loved prophet and teacher who has gone on to be with the Lord, taught on these principles and stressed the importance of not engaging with these principalities:

"To attack principalities and powers over a geographic area is as useless as throwing hatchets at the moon and leaves you open to unforeseen and unperceived attacks... Our warfare is against personal attacks on earth, not principalities. That which affects the earth...our focus is to change mindsets and hearts...principalities have the right to be there (because of corporate mindsets and beliefs). It's our heart that determines what rules in the second heaven. We don't tear it down unless we tear down the high places in our own hearts first." —**John Paul Jackson** in the 2014 video *The Mystery of Spiritual Warfare*

Through the years I have been to many prayer gatherings in various settings where intercessors have taken up their swords to come against principalities and territorial spirits with great fervor and passion. Thinking this was how to use their spiritual authority to defeat the enemy, I have seen countless warriors in prayer spend the majority of their time waving their swords and rebuking the devil. Though there was never a doubt about their love for the Lord, their zeal for the Church, and a sincere desire to see people set free, the protocol was simply unbiblical. Yet, this is the model that has been practiced over and over again. It's time we go back to the Word of God to dig deeper concerning these weapons of our warfare and how to engage the enemy—or not.

Practices from the Early Church

In the book of Acts, there are numerous examples that illustrate how the apostles dealt with city-wide strongholds. They never rebuked a principality or staged a demonstration against the city officials. Their methods were always the same: preach and teach the good news in order to change the way the people think (see Acts 4:29-30, 5:40-42, 14:1, 17:16-17). They knew that if public opinion changed toward the truth of the gospel and the Fear of the Lord, the corporate strongholds of witchcraft, rebellion, and deception would lose its hold and the demonic stronghold would be broken.

One story, in particular, demonstrates this principle very clearly. The story is told of Philip going to Samaria where Simon, a sorcerer, had put the entire city under his spell:

Now for some time a man named Simon had practiced sorcery in the city and amazed all the people of Samaria. He boasted that he was someone great, and all the people, both high and low, gave him their attention and exclaimed, "This man is the divine power known as the Great Power." They followed him because he had amazed them for a long time with his magic. But when they believed Philip as he preached the good news of the kingdom of God and the name of Jesus Christ, they were baptized, both men and women. Simon himself believed and was baptized. And he followed Philip everywhere, astonished by the great signs and miracles he saw (Acts 8:9-13 NIV).

Simon was a false prophet producing counterfeit signs and wonders. As a result, the entire city came into deception and fell under a territorial spirit of witchcraft. However, there is no indication that Philip rebuked a principality or led a campaign against Simon. Instead, he preached the good news of Jesus Christ to the masses. He spoke directly to the people in order to change their minds. Because the people believed and their hearts turned toward the Lord, the spirit of witchcraft was broken and Simon, himself, was able to receive the truth of the gospel.

This is a powerful example of public opinion changing, thus disempowering and displacing the enemy's influence. Instead of just sweeping the house clean of demonic intrusion, Philip taught the people how to fill their hearts and minds with lasting truth that attracted heaven instead of hell.

When mindsets are changed and the truth is revealed, the enemy's hold is broken (see 2 Thessalonians 2:10-12). The power and authority of preaching and teaching the good news of Jesus, followed by signs and wonders, was the standard practice of the early disciples. It repeatedly brought results, not only in personal lives, but in shifting an entire city and region toward the Lord.

We must remind ourselves of the primary mission we have as the Ekklesia. It is to demonstrate and extend the Kingdom of God by bringing the lost to salvation and maturing the Body of Christ to reach and impact our culture for Christ. This should always be our goal and our focus. When the enemy opposes this, we raise up the standard and press on.

Many times, demonic influence manifests through the people who have come into agreement with that ungodly belief or practice—whether they know it or not. Following Pentecost, the disciples continually confronted opposition from the spiritual rulers of cities. In the early Church, it was the High Priests, Pharisees, and other spiritual rulers who, through their words and actions, reflected the influence of the demonic spiritual authorities over their cities. These examples illustrate the various ways the disciples responded while keeping their primary mission central. We can learn from these principles of engagement when confronted by similar enemy opposition today.

They continued to teach and preach, performing signs and wonders...

Acts 4:27-29 – Peter and John went before the council and were threatened, but they continued to *teach and preach the truth, followed by signs and wonders.* They responded by asking the Lord for greater boldness to speak His Word—not fight or attack the spiritual rulers of the city.

Acts 5:17-21 – When the spiritual rulers rose up to arrest the disciples, an angel released them from jail and told them to *stand in the temple and speak the words of life*—not pray "against" something.

Acts 5:40-42 – After they were beaten for testifying of Jesus, the disciples *rejoiced and did not cease teaching and preaching* the good news of Jesus.

Acts 14:1-7 – The spiritual rulers at Iconium stirred up trouble for Paul and Barnabas, seeking to stone them. But the disciples *performed signs and wonders and brought many people to the Lord.*

Acts 17:16 – Paul was provoked at the idolatry in the city—a citywide stronghold. He *reasoned in the synagogue* against the mindsets that had given room to the idolatry. Same thing in Acts 18:4.

They ministered peace in the chaos...

Acts 5:33-35 – The spiritual rulers of the city were enraged at the testimony of the disciples. But Gamaliel stood up and *invoked peace,* dismantling the fury.

Acts 19:28-41 – The people of the city became *enraged* and the city was filled with *confusion* when news spread of the disciples teaching against the idolatry in the city. It was Demetrius, a county clerk, who *quieted the spirit of confusion through reason* (Acts 19:39-41). After the uproar ceased, Paul left. The community-wide "attack" was silenced.

They operated in the gifts of Holy Spirit...

Acts 6:8-15 – When Stephen was brought before the council with charges of treason, *"...they could not withstand the **wisdom and the Spirit** with which he was speaking."*

Acts 7:51-53 – At the end of his speech, Stephen prophetically revealed their sin. He did not pronounce final judgment or verbally attack them. Rather, under the unction of the Holy Spirit, he boldly spoke God's truth.

Acts 9:36-43 – In Joppa, Paul ministered a gift of healing to Tabitha (Dorcas) and the entire city was reached through the miracle.

They left, waiting for a better time...

Acts 9:23-25 – When Saul was under a death threat, the disciples didn't fight the system—they escaped. They knew better than to draw attention—and an unnecessary fight.

Acts 9:28-31 – When the Hellenists of Damascus sought to kill Barnabas, the disciples came and took him away to keep the peace, until the city was ready for deliverance. It said the church was being built up and learning to walk in the Fear of the Lord.

Acts 13:48-52 – Paul and the disciples were seeing many conversions to Christ in Antioch. But the Jews incited the *"...devout women of high standing and the leading men of the city"*—spiritual authorities—and stirred up persecution, driving Paul and Barnabas out of the city. They *"shook off the dust from their feet"* and left for Iconium, filled with joy and with the Holy Spirit.

Acts 17 – The confrontation in Thessalonica demonstrated, again, that the disciples were not looking to pick a fight. Their goal was to establish proper spiritual authority through the Church and proclaim the Kingdom of God. This was a repeated pattern of the disciples; when strife was stirred up, they would leave the city so as not to stir up any more trouble until proper spiritual authority of the Church had been established.

They prayed...

Acts 12:4-19 – Peter was supernaturally released from prison after Herod planned to kill him. The saints who prayed for him didn't fight or stand up to the rulers, demanding his release. They prayed for his freedom and he was released by an angel and then quietly left the city.

Acts 16:6-10 – Through a prophetic word, the Holy Spirit forbade Paul to go into Macedonia. Then the Spirit of Jesus would not allow him to go into Bithynia. Rather than assuming their authority could take them anywhere, the disciples always prayed and waited for the green light from the Spirit.

They appealed to the people...

Acts 13:4-12 – Paul confronted the magician, Elymas. Under the unction of the Holy Spirit, Paul prophetically exposed the sin of Elymas. He didn't command him to stop—he appealed to him: *"...will you not stop making crooked the straight paths of the Lord?"* His hope was to win Elymas over. He prophesied a sign, blindness, in order to get Elymas to believe. As a result, the proconsul who was watching believed at the *"teaching of the Lord."*

Acts 16:11-24 – When Paul and Silas entered Philippi, rather than going directly to the city square to preach, they went to a leading citizen of the city, Lydia. Knowing her influence among the people, they shared the gospel with her and she got saved along with her entire household, thus opening the door to the city.

Acts 19:8-10 – Paul spoke for months in the synagogue teaching about the Kingdom of God. When rebels started to stir up dissension, he left and focused on those who were ready to hear the Word. *"This continued for two years so that all the residents of Asia heard the word of the Lord."* The disciples looked for good ground—those who were spiritually hungry—not necessarily the crowds.

They allowed sin to take its course...

Acts 19:11-17 – When the sons of Sceva tried to invoke the name of Jesus for personal gain, they ended up being destroyed by the very demons they were trying to exorcise. The Lord used even the false prophets to release a Fear of the Lord on the people, without any help from the disciples.

They recognized the power of jurisdictional authority...

Acts 22 – Paul in Jerusalem stirred up the anger of the Jews when their sins became evident through his preaching. However, when the authorities of the city tried to bind and flog him, they learned he was a Roman citizen. They had to release him because he knew the authority he had in his own "field" and exercised his jurisdictional rights.

Acts 23:12 – The Jews made a vow—binding themselves by an ungodly oath which is a form of witchcraft—to kill Paul. He was rescued by a Roman centurion, having learned he was a Roman citizen; again, due to his legal jurisdiction in the land.

They established the Church with healthy leadership...

Acts 14:19-23 – Paul and Barnabas returned to Iconium and Antioch, encouraging and building up the churches there, knowing that it would be a process to see the spiritual authorities of the city diminish in power and control. They appointed elders with prayer and fasting and dedicated them to the Lord. This was a priority in order to *displace* the ungodly spiritual rulership of the city. *Until spiritual authority was established in the Church, they did not engage those who opposed them.*

They knew the power of corporate agreement...

Acts 18:9-10 – Jesus commanded Paul, *"Do not be afraid, but go on speaking and do not be silent, for I am with you and no one will attack you to harm you, for I have many in this city who are my people."* Jesus indicated the importance of a corporate presence in a city in order to bring ultimate freedom from demonic strongholds.

Important Principles

From this brief overview in Acts, we can glean some important principles:

1. There was no indication of "spiritual warfare" in "coming against" demonic strongholds of a city or region.

2. The priority was always preaching the Kingdom of God and changing mindsets of the people.

3. The disciples focused on winning souls to Jesus, knowing that their changed allegiance would disempower the principalities over their city.

4. Long-term history of the cities show that as the churches grew and godly leadership matured, the atmosphere of the city changed, and more people came to salvation as a result. (Also notice the eventual shift of cities as the apostles

matured believers and established godly government in the churches.)

5. Spiritual authority has its boundaries. Even the disciples were not "allowed" to go into certain regions at times, without even knowing why.

6. Paul appealed to the spiritual rulers of cities and regions. His ultimate goal was to win them over by the truths of the Kingdom, not to engage in a confrontation of power.

7. When there were times of spiritual confrontation, the disciples downplayed them or avoided them, seeking first to save the individuals afflicted.

8. Any spiritual oppression or blockage from territorial spirits was dealt with through prayer and ongoing discipleship to bring long-term displacement of the demonic stronghold.

Praying on the High Places

Though there are no New Testament examples of this, I do know of instances where groups of intercessors have gone to "high places" within a region to pray against long-standing demonic strongholds in an area. These may be mountaintops or known spiritual gateways in a region.

Drawing from Old Testament examples of such confrontation—such as Elijah and the prophets of Baal—some intercessors feel empowered to confront these principalities head-on. I am not suggesting there may not be strategic times when the Lord authorizes such prayer, but they are few and far between. There is evidence of some fruit due to these kinds of prayer initiatives when done in the right spirit in conjunction with local leaders. But, we cannot assume this to be a first response. Nor should we presume upon our authority to use this method of warfare.

Given the examples and common practices within the early Church following Pentecost, we must evaluate this kind of prayer initiative by carefully considering these key factors:

- Are the recognized spiritual shepherds in that region in agreement with this prayer initiative and praying together with the intercessors?

  - It is imperative that intercessors work alongside the pastors and apostolic leaders in an area if there is to be unified prayer with any spiritual authority. This is probably *the* most important factor in having the needed authority to complete such a prayer assignment. Because it is a corporate stronghold, it requires corporate agreement with authorized leadership, not just an intercessory unction or prophetic proclamation.

  - Intercessors are called to support and undergird the work of the local church and its leaders, not the other way around. Primary spiritual authority for any region has been given to the appointed five-fold ministers and elders who are actively engaged in and connected to the local body. Without their support, encouragement, and added counsel, any prayer initiative addressing a territorial spirit will be ineffective. Worse yet, it will stir up things in the spirit without adequate spiritual covering and corporate agreement in prayer.

  - It will be most effective when *local* intercessors and leaders respond to any heaven-sent initiative and pray in the "high places." Those who already live in a community have the added authority to speak over that land. Though the Lord may send a five-fold minister to a region to encourage, equip, and partner with such an initiative, the local citizens face the task of stewarding the issue long-term. (This is also an important consideration when intercessors visit communities other than their own and share a "word" or revelation for prayer. Though they may provide some needed insight, it is still the local intercessors who will have the greatest impact in stewarding the breakthrough.)

- Has there been sufficient times of repentance, both personal and corporate, in order to remove any legal foothold the enemy may have in disqualifying such prayer?

  – I have witnessed intercessors demanding a corporate religious spirit to submit to them when they themselves are walking in a similar spirit of pride due to their prophetic revelations. I have heard others pray against idolatry when they are enamored by certain Bible teachers and celebrity preachers, unwilling to listen to other perspectives. In our zeal to pray, let's not become blind to the ways in which we may be operating in the same spirit.

  – Before we can "take authority" over any spiritual power, we must evaluate our legal status in the spirit, specifically our own walk and history. This is where "courtroom prayer" is most important. I believe this is the approach most needed in the "high places." We must be willing to present a clear case and take any responsibility for ways in which we are fueling the problem so that all legal rights to the enemy can be nullified and rendered powerless. Rather than a confrontation of power, this should be a confrontation with the Truth.

— Though we should personally "take every thought captive," we are not responsible to take every *corporate* thought captive. The strongholds we are to demolish start with our own (see 2 Corinthians 10:4-5). If every believer in a community of faith would take this seriously on a personal level and walk in true freedom, our corporate authority would be off the charts!

- Is there a strategy in place for changing mindsets, walking in the opposite spirit, and discipling the local church for long-term freedom?

  — We dare not try to sweep the house clean if we have nothing to put in its place (see Matthew 12:43-45). We must be aware of the lies and half-truths that opened the door to the territorial spirit in the first place. Without proper teaching and further discipling of the people on the land, any seeming breakthrough may be short-lived.

Conclusion

Seeing the long-term goal of establishing a city for the Lord, our goal needs to be on praying for the lost, preaching the good news of the Kingdom, discipling sons and daughters, and bringing heaven to earth. It's not simply *getting* free from demonic influence and oppression, but *staying* free, that matters. Our charge is to guard, keep, and occupy the territory the Lord wants to give us so that Kingdom rule can be established, not for short-term relief, but for long-term transformation.

The most powerful weapon we have in defeating our spiritual adversary is the gospel of the Kingdom. Regardless of the warfare around us, we are called to be the dread champions of the King. We have been filled and empowered by the Spirit for one primary purpose, and that is to know Him and to make Him known. It is only when the culture around us sees a living demonstration of that Kingdom at work that the lies and counterfeits of enemy occupation will be broken. Through our prayers, proclamations, and supernatural manifestations of His love, we can destroy the works of the enemy and make room for His presence to reign.

PRAYER GUIDE

SHIFTING
the SPIRITUAL
AUTHORITY
Over CITIES

Seek the Lord concerning these issues in your own city and region:

Cleansing of any idolatry or double-mindedness: (1 John 2:16; James 1:8; Ezekiel 36:26-27).

> *Lord, forgive us for the idols in our land. We confess we have looked to fleshly attractions and entertainment, people of title and fame, and the accumulation of worldly goods instead of You. (Repent of any specific place, person, or thing that has become an idol.)*
>
> *Cleanse us for being divided in our hearts and minds and give us an undivided heart that we might serve You wholly and without reserve. Wash us with Your Word and give us a new spirit that would cause us to walk in Your ways.*

The Fear of the Lord to be upon the city: (James 1:17; Proverbs 14:26; Jeremiah 32:38-41; Psalm 25:12-14).

We choose to live in the Fear of the Lord and not the fear of man. We pledge, O God, to fear Your name above all others and to look to You as the only Source of life, liberty, and every good thing.

Lord, give us a singleness of heart and action so that we will always Fear the Lord for our own good and the good of our children.

May the Fear of the Lord rest upon our families, our churches, our businesses and schools, our government, and every sector of our city so that it may go well with us and that Your covenant will stand secure.

The angelic host to accomplish their assignments: (Psalm 34:7; Psalm 91:11; Hebrews 12:22).

Father, we thank You for the angels that You have sent to aid and assist us in this battle. We ask for and acknowledge their presence in our city to guard, keep, and protect every citizen from harm.

We bless their assignments to war against any enemy of the Kingdom and to push back the forces of evil on our behalf. We thank You that this battle is not ours, but Yours.

The altar of His presence to be established: (Ezekiel 37:26-28; Isaiah 66:1; Psalm 27:8).

Lord, establish our city as a dwelling place of Your presence, a light in the darkness, and a refuge for the lost.

Raise up prayer and worship altars across our region that will continually offer sacrifices of praise and thanksgiving to welcome Your rule and reign on this land.

Expose and remove any and every idolatrous place of worship that attracts the darkness and render their altars ineffective and powerless.

We dedicate ourselves to daily seek Your face and know Your heart for the sake of Your Kingdom.

The peace of the Lord to overshadow the land: (Mark 4:39; Exodus 33:14; Psalm 91:1; Isaiah 9:6).

*We speak **peace** to every storm the enemy tries to stir up and we speak **peace** to every heart that is troubled.*

We declare our community to be a city of peace and rest and reject and resist any spirit of agitation, fear, or violence that seeks entry.

We declare the goodness of God and the rule of heaven to overshadow and displace every work of darkness that seeks to steal, kill, and destroy our faith in God. Greater is He who is in us than he that is in the world.

We decree the Prince of Peace as ruler of our land and that the government will rest on His shoulders of which there will be no end.

The establishment of godly leadership: (Exodus 18:21; Proverbs 16:7; Hebrews 13:7; 2 Timothy 2:15).

Father, we ask for godly leadership to be firmly established in our community and for every counterfeit, rebel, and traitor to be removed. We ask that those who have been called and appointed for leadership in this hour to be revealed, acknowledged, and affirmed, rightly positioned and placed in the fields You have assigned them.
We speak blessing on every shepherd in our city whose heart is fully yielded to You and ask for an increase of grace and favor in their lives.
May every sector in our community be influenced and guided by leaders who are fully aligned with Your heart and purposes.

The wisdom and knowledge of the Lord to be revealed: (Daniel 2:21-22; 1 Corinthians 2:7-10).

Lord, give us Your wisdom, knowledge, and understanding to reveal and expose the hidden things of darkness to bring them into the light. By Your Spirit, teach us Your ways to rightly discern between good and evil that we might walk in truth and integrity.
Mature us as Your sons and daughters to be ambassadors of Your Kingdom and representatives of heaven. May we operate in increased wisdom and discernment that would attract nonbelievers and demonstrate the power and authority of Your Kingdom.
Father, we declare our community to be under the lordship of Christ and under the rule of heaven that You might be known and that every knee will bow and every tongue confess that You, alone, are God. In Jesus' name. Amen.

Chapter 10

From
REFORMATION *to*
TRANSFORMATION

From Vision to Reality

As we consider the potential to change the atmosphere over entire cities and regions through our prayers and actions, there is one example in the United States that demonstrates the power of some of these principles. It was in a small Kentucky town where God did a supernatural work, starting in 2004. It was because believers came together and prayed for one united purpose—to unseat a demonic ruling authority in their region and save their city. The incredible breakthrough and transformation story of Manchester, Kentucky, has been seen by thousands in Sentinel Group's 2010 documentary film, *An Appalachian Dawn*. I believe their story illustrates what can happen at the local level when the Church begins to engage in both unified prayer and a readiness to act. I also believe their journey to transformation is a "first fruits" testimony of what can happen again—even on a national level.

From Corruption to Supernatural Transformation

Manchester is a small town in Clay County, Kentucky, historically known for its salt mines and generational feuding. Due to a long history of corruption, political control, and family hostilities, this small town eventually became a poverty-ridden magnet for drugs and crime, known nationally as the painkiller capital of the United States. By the time the new millennium started, it was the kids of the "good folks" who were dying from drug overdoses, suicides, and caught in a trap of addiction and hopelessness. This crisis compelled the small number of believers in this town to band together in prayer to break off the spirit of death hanging over their community and their children.

Doug Abner was a local Charismatic pastor who walked through this journey with the help of a fellow Baptist minister, Ken Bolin. Pastor Doug shared how his relationship with Pastor Ken was unusual to begin with. Their differing theological bents and methods of ministry would normally be huge barriers in forging any kind of partnership. And yet, because of their common concern for their community, these two godly men laid down their personal preferences and religious ideologies in order to lead their small town through the growing crisis. They ended up being best friends and unwavering prayer partners.

By the late 1990s, the drug problem had become so big in Manchester that one local lawbreaker had a drive-through window at his home where up to 600 cars a day would drive through to obtain illegal drugs and alcohol. This emboldened criminal also had more than a dozen elected officials on his payroll, buying their protection and silence.

Even the local elections were bought and paid for, making it impossible for anyone outside the local ring of power to run for office or bring any positive change. The dark coalition of drug-runners, criminals, and politicians had knit a tight web around Manchester, but Pastor Doug and

Pastor Ken were committed to praying for these strongholds to be broken and the city set free.

In 1999 they brought together several other churches in the community to bring the John Jacobs Power Team to schools. The pastors even began to pray together. Due to the success of that outreach, they realized their potential in working together. By 2003, one death a week was attributed to illegal drugs. That year Pastor Ken, a man who hadn't given much credence to the gifts of the Spirit, had a prophetic dream about doing a march through town. This unexpected sign seemed to solidify the unity and strength of the core group that had been meeting regularly to pray.

Pastor Doug said that people became so desperate for change that even nonbelievers heard about their Saturday morning prayer meetings and started to come. At times, more than one hundred people would be praying, repenting, and weeping on a Saturday morning, being of one mind and heart for the sake of their community. When Pastor Ken had the dream about the march, they knew it was God and planned to walk through the center of Manchester to take a stand for their city on Sunday, May 2, 2004.

They were not without enemies, however. The drug lords and corrupt politicians heard what they were doing and began to issue death threats. Months before the planned march, both pastors received numerous threats on their lives, their churches, and their families. Their faith was secure, however, and their resolve was firm. Pastor Doug reported, "We had a saying in Manchester that as bad as the darkness was, the lack of the light was much more of a problem. When the good people sit back and do nothing, evil prevails."

That Sunday, May 2, turned out to be cold and rainy and the streets appeared empty. The organizers knew that if there was not a large turnout, the idea was a bust. Even by 3:00 in the afternoon, the clouds and wet conditions seemed to be winning and they began to wonder if they missed God. But then, church busses and vans started pouring in and within a short time, they were shocked to find sixty-three churches represented with an estimated 3,500-4,000 people marching through town. The mass of people that showed up represented roughly 20 percent of the entire county population. By the time they all marched to the park for a service, the atmosphere was charged with a collective unity and boldness that was tangible.

When the sixty-three pastors openly repented for their apathy and lack of leadership in the public park, something powerful broke. The Fear of the Lord fell upon the crowd gathered and the tangible presence of God moved in. Everyone could tell something had changed. Many were on their faces in repentance and worship. A power and peace enveloped them that would end up carrying them through the challenging weeks and months ahead.

Though it would take almost three years for all the corruption to be uncovered and crooked officials brought to justice, their community saw incredible results. "The March Seen Around the World" became a testimony around the globe. The combination of their persistent prayers, covenant relationships, and Spirit-led demonstration opened the way for heaven to move in and do what no individual could take credit for.

Not only was the march itself historic, but the subsequent changes and turnarounds of this city and neighboring community took everyone by surprise. Soon after the march, instead of criticizing the corrupt officials and openly accusing them of wrongdoing, the prayer teams went to the offices of these same city officials with gifts of potted plants and asked if they could pray for them. One of these corrupt officials had previously threatened a pastor and his church. To their amazement, this official called in his staff and allowed Pastor Doug to lead them in prayer. Years later, this same official would confess Jesus as Lord and ask forgiveness for what he had done.

The Fear of the Lord was so prevalent, those involved in illegal activities began to turn on each other. As believers continued to pray, God battled on their behalf. Within three years, more than 3,300 drug dealers were arrested with a 97 percent conviction rate. A coalition of citizens, churches, and law enforcement called UNITE formed to tackle the drug problem together. Pastors were invited into police precincts to minister to offenders as soon as they were arrested. Even with ongoing opposition, churches in the community began to see a dramatic increase of salvations and the favor of God came upon the local church.

Pastor Doug shares that the book of Nehemiah became their blueprint for how to rebuild their community. They were not swayed by the criticism of their opponents nor did they give in to the threats and insults (see Nehemiah 4:7-9). Instead, they sought the Lord's strategies, worked together, and got involved. With permission from the State Attorney General, Pastor Doug's church began to televise previously closed-door courtroom proceedings for accountability to the public.

In 2006, they championed a "Promote the Vote" campaign to encourage local citizens to run for office. The event ran all day as 130 ordinary citizens, many of them believers, ran for office. In 2007, a Christian woman was voted in as mayor and the community saw even more dramatic changes as she, along with other newly elected officials, began to lead the city with godly wisdom and creative strategies for growth. Churches began to offer recovery programs for drug addicts and a Teen Challenge Center was established where lifelong destructive cycles were broken. The prayers of the saints were put into action and God-fearing believers were having increased influence and impact as they engaged with their community to bring positive change. Their decade-long transformation process was truly miraculous.

What if Manchester is a forerunner for the nation? What if their story is but a small illustration of what can happen for an entire country—is even now happening in our nation? Regardless of the strongholds, the principles are the same. Though their breakthrough moment on May 2, 2004, went viral, their journey was not an overnight success. It took years of building relationships, persistent prayer, and a vision for their corporate future. It was their determination to work together for a greater cause that empowered them to take, keep, and occupy their territory for the glory of God.

Pastor Doug said it was not always easy. The first few years were a challenge as many illegal activities continued, even in the midst of revival. Even so, God's tangible presence gave the people a boldness to confront the challenges. They didn't get caught up in opinions and avoided any negative statements about their city. Realizing the power of their declarations and the impact of their witness, they chose their battles carefully. Pastors agreed to focus on the non-negotiables—heaven and hell issues—and let the other stuff go. They were intentional in seeking the Lord together, knowing the true power of unity in defeating their enemies. Their journey was similar to that of the Israelites in possessing the promised land as they took one step at a time: *"Little by little I will drive them out before you, until you have increased and possess the land"* (Exodus 23:30).

Not only were the people changed, even the land began to change from the forests and animals to the water itself. For approximately the next ten years, Manchester, now known as the "City of Hope," would see phenomenal change and transformation as the people worked together.

Unfortunately, the momentum didn't last.

My husband and I visited Manchester in 2015 with a team from Intercessors for America and George Otis Jr., the producer of the transformation documentaries. We spent a few days with Pastor Doug and some of the leaders to learn more of what happened so we could share some of these truths with leaders and intercessors around the nation. By this time, Pastor Doug indicated that the believers had become so used to God's favor and grace during the years of transformation, they stopped praying.

They let down their guard and began to assume the change would last. He said that was their biggest mistake—not continuing in steadfast prayer.

By the time we visited, a new mayor had been elected and he was not a believer. Old ways were beginning to emerge again, and many of the pastors who had been involved in the march during the early days had moved on. Though the political corruption was thwarted, the drug problems were minimal, and the community at large was relatively healthy, there were signs of apathy and disconnect among believers.

Pastor Doug and his wife, Linda, were already seeking the Lord in how to reignite the passion for prayer and the vision for long-term transformation. They had been traveling and sharing the story of Manchester and eventually opened the Appalachian Center for Transformation to share the vision with those who passed through. Even so, they realized there was much work yet to do.

More recently, Pastor Doug reflected on their experiences, and shared some of the critical mistakes made in their journey. He said that when Manchester began to draw international attention, he and his wife, along with numerous other community leaders, began to travel to share their story. Unfortunately, they didn't realize that in going, they had left a back door open. Without raising up solid leadership at home, it was just a matter of time before old patterns and mindsets began to emerge. They hadn't realized how important it was to teach the next generation about their history and the values and lessons they had learned.

The other downfall was that they hadn't done enough in mentoring and discipling families. Due to the generational strongholds from decades past, lingering habits and unhealthy patterns went unchecked. Though signs, wonders, and miracles were happening on a consistent basis, the values and mindsets of families in the community did not change enough to guarantee a healthy succession. In their zeal for sharing their story with the world, they had forgotten to keep the fires burning at home and to raise up healthy sons and daughters to carry the vision. They realized without healthy families and godly leadership, no miraculous intervention could last.

In January of 2019, they opened the Regional Prayer Centre on Main Street. Their passion and vision for total transformation of Manchester continues as they seek the Lord for new strategies in this new season. God is already responding to their heart cries and drawing fresh faces with hungry hearts for this next phase of Manchester's story of redemption. Many believe that God is going to visit Manchester again, and Pastor Doug and his wife are committed to the long-term building process to ensure a ready place for God to come and dwell.

I believe what happened to Manchester is happening to the United States. The defining 2016 election of Donald Trump to the presidency was, considered by many, a miracle. Though many had been praying for heaven's intervention, by all accounts, the spiritual storms and bleak predictions seemed to indicate a lost cause. And yet, just as the cloud fell in Manchester city park, so did God's grace move in on election night, granting us an unexpected victory and renewed hope for the future. The breakthrough emboldened many to start confronting the corruption in high places that had taken our nation hostage. But, just as Manchester learned, it is a long road to recovery and restoration that will require ongoing and fervent prayer, and discipling future generations in the ways of the Lord in order to secure our national inheritance.

God Is Speaking to Cities!

Most Christians are so caught up in their own personal lives and the close circle of friends they have, it's hard to get in touch with the needs of a city. And yet, God is stirring hearts all around this nation to do just that. Community prayer groups have been on the rise and many corporate gatherings and prayer initiatives are being launched within countless cities to take a stand for righteousness in their own territory. The moral crises we face, the increased corruption in government, and the rising tide of socialist ideologies have caused even nonbelievers to rise up and speak out. The Lord is using the increased godless agenda to call us to action and to prayer.

The reality is that national transformation can only happen when there is a cumulative effect of individual cities and regions both taking and occupying their land. National leadership is always homegrown, and it's at the local level that change must start. The more communities that understand these principles and practice them consistently, the more likely we will be as a nation to not only displace wicked rulers, but have the needed influence and authority to govern our land the way God has always intended.

God's vision is big and He is calling out to cities to take a stand for righteousness and become communities of refuge and dwelling places for His presence. The only thing that will hinder Him from moving in our community is us. We are the ones who must take ownership in this call and take action.

> *Then he began to denounce the cities where most of his mighty works had been done, because they did not repent. "Woe to you, Chorazin! Woe to you, Bethsaida! For if the mighty works done in you had been done in Tyre and Sidon, they would have repented long ago in sackcloth and ashes. But I tell you, it will be more bearable on the day of judgment for Tyre and Sidon than for you. And you, Capernaum, will you be exalted to heaven?"* (Matthew 11:20-23)

Just as in Manchester, it always starts with repentance and taking responsibility for the sins on the land. The wonderful promise is that if we are faithful to do this and commit ourselves to obeying His voice and engaging with our culture, He will entrust us with even more so that His Kingdom can continue to increase and expand.

> *And he said to him, "Well done, good servant! Because you have been faithful in a very little, you shall have authority over ten cities"* (Luke 19:17).

Alan Vincent, an apostolic father and prophetic voice to the nations, speaks to believers about the spiritual authority we've been given and how we must use it at the community level. He wrote about this in his book, *Kingdom at War:*

"There is power in intercession. We need intercessors who can clearly hear God and then, through their prayers and the right God-directed activism, get into the realms of politics, the judiciary, law enforcement, education, and the media so His Kingdom can truly come."

"The kingdom of satan has long been established on Earth and is still here until the Kingdom of God comes to forcibly replace it. There is no vacant, neutral territory anywhere in the world. Therefore, every attempt to establish the Kingdom of God is automatically an invasion of what satan has illegally occupied and now regards as his territory. That is why the Kingdom of God always suffers violence and is vigorously attacked the moment it appears to be gaining ground. The only way to deal with that demonic violence is to be even more spiritually violent in our response.[1]"

God doesn't just want to fix our problems, He wants to totally transform us. This isn't just about governing well, but living well. It is about stewarding all that God has given us so that others can see a living demonstration of heaven on earth. This is God's desire that started in the Garden. He has always desired for us to steward this land for His glory. The only thing that can thwart this plan, is us.

When we were in Manchester with George Otis Jr., my husband and I learned more about the many communities he had documented that had experienced a supernatural transformation birthed through prayer. In every case, it appeared that a crisis or major threat caused the people to gather and pray. We finally asked him, "Has there ever been an example where hunger for God, alone, drew this kind of response?" We wanted to know if there always had to be a threat before something supernatural happened.

His answer? "Not that I know of." He said that, unfortunately, human nature is to put off any serious pursuit of God until there's a crisis. Especially when it is a national crisis, people won't take any action until it gets personal. My husband and I pondered this and began to pray that perhaps, someday, there would be a people hungry enough for God that their passion for His presence would be greater than their need for a rescue.

Endnote

1. Alan Vincent, *The Kingdom at War: Using Intercessory Prayer to Dispel the Darkness* (Shippensburg, PA: Destiny Image Publishers, 2011).

PRAYER GUIDE

PREPARING YOUR CITY *for* TRANSFORMATION

Lift up praise and worship over the city.

Extol the Lord, Jerusalem; praise your God, Zion. He strengthens the bars of your gates and blesses your people within you (Psalm 147:12-13 NIV).

- Magnify the name of Jesus above all other names (Luke 10:17; Philippians 2:9-11).

- Declare His lordship in your community and region (2 Kings 19:19; Psalm 50:23).

- Read psalms of praise to displace any voices of darkness (Psalm 33,35,65,67).

Declare your home and community to be a dwelling place for God's presence.

> *And I will be to her a wall of fire all around, declares the Lord, and I will be the glory in her midst* (Zechariah 2:5).

- Celebrate the light of His presence that brings strength and favor (Psalm 89:15-17).

- Praise Him for His presence that disarms the enemy (Psalm 31:20; Exodus 33:14).

- Thank God for His presence that prevents any deception or falsehood from taking hold (Psalm 101:7).

- Invite the Fear of the Lord to rest upon your community (Psalm 34:7; Isaiah 8:13-14).

Call for unity in the church and oneness of spirit among spiritual leaders.

> *And I am no longer in the world, but they are in the world, and I am coming to you. Holy Father, keep them in your name, which you have given me, that they may be one, even as we are one* (John 17:11).

- Pray that the hearts of leaders would be drawn together by a oneness of spirit (Ephesians 4:16; Galatians 3:26-28).

- Pray that doctrinal differences would give way to demonstrating the power of the gospel (2 Chronicles 30:12; 1 Corinthians 1:10).

- Pray that a unified voice would arise from the city, reflecting the Father's heart and will (Romans 15:5-6).

- Pray that believers would be drawn together in the power of covenant community (Acts 18:9-10).

Disarm any plans of the enemy to threaten, harm, or hijack the citizens or territory.

...Do not be afraid and do not be dismayed at this great horde, for the battle is not yours but God's (2 Chronicles 20:15).

- Declare God's righteous boundaries around the city (Psalm 31:20; Jeremiah 5:22).

- Renounce—refuse to recognize—and cancel any threats of harm or property damage (Isaiah 63:9; Luke 4:28-30).

- Pray that communications of the enemy would be confused and canceled (Jeremiah 20:11-12; Psalm 55:9-10).

- Counter negative words or curses spoken with the promises of God (Psalm 109:26-31; 2 Corinthians 10:2-6).

Declare that the light of Truth will dispel any darkness and expose the lies.

In him was life, and that life was the light of all mankind. The light shines in the darkness, and the darkness has not overcome it (John 1:4-5 NIV).

- Bless the city with an increased awareness of His presence and truth that dispels darkness (Psalm 36:9).

- Pray that those who oppose God's heart and ways would encounter Jesus (Acts 8:12-13).

- Pray that counterfeits would be exposed, bringing the Fear of the Lord (Acts 19:14-17).

- Pray that every evil practice would collide with Truth and Life (Acts 8:4-8).

Speak God's blessings and protection over transportation and communication lines.

The Lord will cause your enemies who rise against you to be defeated before you. They shall come out against you one way and flee before you seven ways (Deuteronomy 28:7).

- Pray protection over city streets and citizens young and old (Psalm 121:8; Proverbs 10:9).

- Bless the roadways and highways with the holiness of God (Isaiah 35:8-10).

- Declare the roadways consecrated unto the Lord to bring wandering souls back to Him (Jeremiah 50:5).

Pray for the Word of God and message of the cross to be shared with power.

For I will give you a mouth and wisdom, which none of your adversaries will be able to withstand or contradict. ...You will be hated by all for my name's sake. But not a hair of your head will perish. By your endurance you will gain your lives (Luke 21:15, 17-19).

- Declare that the power of God's Word and anointing of the Holy Spirit would disarm the adversary (Acts 6:9-10; 2 Thessalonians 1:5-7).

- Pray for boldness to declare the truth of the gospel (Acts 4:29-31; Philippians 1:14).

- Pray that the Spirit of truth would be proclaimed and heard (John 16:13-14).

- Declare the favor of God on those who preach and teach the Word of God (Acts 17:16-17,32).

Thank God for His delivering power in defeating all His enemies.

Little children, you are from God and have overcome them, for he who is in you is greater than he who is in the world (1 John 4:4).

Chapter 11

The MORDECAI MANDATE

Securing Your City

Principles of Engagement in the Public Square

Through my years of intercession, I have learned the power of the hidden place and the call to intercession in secret. God is not always looking for those with national platforms and mega-ministries to be world-changers. Many times it starts with one person tucked away in God's presence, far away from the crowds and headlines.

I believe many will be surprised when we get to heaven and find all the hidden men and women of God who dramatically altered history because of their prayers, even though their names were never recognized on this side of the veil. Because of their passion for the Lord and zeal for righteousness, it didn't matter who knew or who saw them; they simply engaged with heaven in declaring God's Word over the field He assigned them. I believe there are those, even now, with a mandate on their lives to alter history from the hidden place of prayer. *You* could be one of them.

We can learn much from one intercessor in the Bible who affected an entire nation through his prayers as well as his actions. Though many are familiar with Esther's role in delivering Israel from annihilation, it was Mordecai who paved the way for this national breakthrough through his prayers and engagement in the public square. His faithful perseverance in the midst of uncertainties and threats show a man with a mandate—an assignment from the Lord. Not only was he faithful in prayer; he was willing to take action, even at personal cost. His faith in God was secure enough to be a conduit of righteousness at a time when the destiny of an entire nation was at risk.

Mordecai's story reveals several key principles for effective prayer and engagement at the community and national level. Study his journey and consider how to apply these principles in your personal intercession, as well as corporate intercession for your community.

Consider how these following ten principles might impact our prayers for the nation and how intercessors can activate their prayers by engaging in the various mountains of our culture:

1. Loving God and Others

> *Mordecai had a cousin named Hadassah, whom he had brought up because she had neither father nor mother. This young woman, who was also known as Esther, had a lovely figure and was beautiful. Mordecai had taken her as his own daughter when her father and mother died* (Esther 2:7 NIV).

Mordecai was a father figure to Esther. In raising her, he helped establish her faith, as well as her love for God and the Jewish people. This bond of fellowship directed their hearts, their prayers, and their responses throughout their journey. They had a covenant relationship with one another formed within a community of faith. This kind of foundation is essential to effective prayer. Meaningful relationships and mutual concern for others helps to establish the proper motivation in prayer. **We must be tied to a community of believers if we are to have the proper motivation, vision, and spiritual authority in prayer.**

2. Going "On-Site for Insight"

Every day he walked back and forth near the courtyard of the harem to find out how Esther was and what was happening to her (Esther 2:11 NIV).

After Esther went to the palace, Mordecai kept close watch over her. He believed he could learn more if he was physically close to where she was. In fact, he was prayer-walking on a daily basis, watching and interceding for Esther! Mordecai was on-site to listen and learn, seeking the Lord for insight during the twelve months of Esther's beauty treatments for the king. **Prayer-walking is a powerful tool of intercession when seeking wisdom and insight concerning things taking place on the land.** Not only can we receive deeper understanding, but our presence and prayers can change the atmosphere (see Genesis 13:17). Especially when praying for governmental issues and challenges in the marketplace, our prayers on-site can make the difference between assumption and secondhand reports, and God-inspired revelation.

3. Engaging in the Public Square

Now when the virgins were gathered together the second time, Mordecai was sitting at the king's gate (Esther 2:19).

Mordecai sat at the "king's gate" where decisions were made, decrees were issued, and verdicts were rendered on behalf of the king and the nation. Whether he was an invited participant or careful observer, he sought to be better informed. He didn't wait for information to come to him; he went to the place where information was shared. **This shows the critical need today for believers to be positioned near our city gates where transactions occur.** Firsthand information is critical to effective prayer. Our influence within our community will grow exponentially when we attend community meetings, interact with city officials, and converse with other citizens who are actively working to better the community.

4. Speaking Out Against Corruption

In those days, as Mordecai was sitting at the king's gate, Bigthan and Teresh, two of the king's eunuchs, who guarded the threshold, became angry and sought to lay hands on King Ahasuerus. And this came to the knowledge of Mordecai, and he told it to Queen Esther, and Esther told the king in the name of Mordecai. When the affair was investigated and found to be so, the men were both hanged on the gallows... (Esther 2:21-23).

Mordecai's decision to sit in this place of political activity proved to be significant. He overheard a plot to assassinate the king and reported it to Esther. He did not let fear stop him from alerting the palace of this threat. When the investigation proved the story to be true, the criminals were hanged, and Mordecai's courageous actions were written in the official record. Believers today need the same level of boldness in confronting wrongdoing or corruption. **Regardless of the threats, our testimonies and actions may be the very catalyst to break the enemy's back.** When we are directed by the Lord and under heaven's protection, we do not have to walk in fear. We can trust the Lord to reveal what is needed and the grace to respond accordingly.

5. Exposing Injustice

And it was recorded in the book of the chronicles in the presence of the king (Esther 2:23).

This seemingly small but significant act granted Mordecai great favor with the king. Unbeknownst to Mordecai or Esther, God planned to use this event to later position Mordecai as a trusted adviser to the king. His willingness to speak up and take action against injustice created a platform for him when much more would be at stake. His actions had been recorded, they made history, and God reminded the king about it when the right time came. Never forsake small beginnings. Your obedience is being recorded in heaven. **God is looking for your faithfulness, no matter how small the task. It may be what opens the door to an even bigger assignment in the future.**

6. Standing in the Face of Intimidation and Threats

And when Haman saw that Mordecai did not bow down or pay homage to him, Haman was filled with fury. But he disdained to lay hands on Mordecai alone. So, as they had made known to him the people of Mordecai, Haman sought to destroy all the Jews, the people of Mordecai, throughout the whole kingdom of Ahasuerus (Esther 3:5-6).

When Mordecai refused to bow to Haman, the demonically driven official sought to kill him. Even so, Mordecai didn't compromise or relent. Despite ridicule and death threats, Mordecai stood his ground and trusted God to vindicate him. It is critical to trust the Lord's timing when seeking justice. **Sometimes, we will be called to simply stand our ground as the Lord makes the next move.** We shouldn't be surprised when there are counterattacks to our actions. Rather, we must see them as opportunities for the Lord to not only vindicate our cause, but trap the enemy.

7. Going Public with Our Cause

When Mordecai learned all that had been done, Mordecai tore his clothes and put on sackcloth and ashes, and went out into the midst of the city, and he cried out with a loud and bitter cry (Esther 4:1).

Once Mordecai learned about the death decree against his people, he humbled himself in front of the whole city in order to bring attention to an injustice. His witness became the example for others to follow throughout the entire province as fellow Jews fasted and wept aloud for their nation. His example is a powerful reminder of our witness and testimony to others. Sometimes, it just takes one radical person to openly pursue the Lord to stir the hearts of others. Don't underestimate what your own obedient response may start. **Others may be looking for direction and your example may be just the thing they need to take action.**

8. Being Informed and Prepared

He also gave him a copy of the text of the edict for their annihilation, which had been published in Susa, to show to Esther and explain it to her, and he told him to instruct her to go into the king's presence to beg for mercy and plead with him for her people (Esther 4:8 NIV).

When asked by an official what he was doing, Mordecai was prepared with a testimony as well as written papers proving his case. His lament was not without cause. He knew the facts and details and was prepared to share them with the appropriate people. We cannot go on secondhand information, rumors, or personal opinions. If we are to have any voice in the public square or influence in governmental affairs, it is imperative that we get the facts straight and share accurate information. **Heaven will back us up when we've done our homework, counted the cost, and come prepared.**

9. Speaking the Word of the Lord

For if you keep silent at this time, relief and deliverance will rise for the Jews from another place, but you and your father's house will perish. And who knows whether you have not come to the kingdom for such a time as this?" (Esther 4:14)

When Esther responded to Mordecai's suggestion of appealing to the king for mercy, she was fearful and hesitant. Yet, his word to her became the key that unlocked the door to her destiny. However, just as Esther was there *"for such a time as this,"* so was Mordecai! Without his presence and prophetic declaration to her, Esther may have missed the God-ordained opportunity before her. You, too, may have a word for someone that will launch them into their assignment. Don't be afraid to speak it. **When the time is ordained by God, the word of the Lord has power to open and shut doors that no one can stop.**

10. Becoming an Ambassador of National Prayer

Then Esther told them to reply to Mordecai, "Go, gather all the Jews to be found in Susa, and hold a fast on my behalf, and do not eat or drink for three days, night or day. I and my young women will also fast as you do. Then I will go to the king, though it is against the law, and if I perish, I perish."

Mordecai then went away and did everything as Esther had ordered him (Esther 4:15-17).

When Mordecai took Esther's request to the Jewish people for a time of national fasting and prayer, he became a conduit of intercession, a messenger of breakthrough. He championed this national call to prayer and stood in the gap for Esther and their people. **Mordecai became a change agent for his nation through prayer and intercession in a time of crisis.**

God is strategically placing believers in every mountain of our culture in order to provide godly leadership in the coming transformation. He is also raising up men and women to come alongside them in prayer. Mordecai was a hidden tool in God's hands, set apart and appointed to influence and direct those in positions of authority. Intercessors can be strategic change agents by not only praying for leaders, but sharing much needed counsel and wisdom to those in high places. Mordecai never sought the throne or center stage but went undercover in prayer and encouragement to one who *was* called there.

We are all called to pray, but I believe there are many who carry the Mordecai Mandate—this commission to stand in the gap, take action, and be an example who will inspire and motivate others to be change agents on the earth.

PRAYER GUIDE

GUARD, KEEP, *and* OCCUPY YOUR CITY

Pray through these following nine principles with other believers in order to come to a oneness of heart and mind concerning the issues in your city and region.

And they all plotted together to come and fight against Jerusalem and to cause confusion in it. And we prayed to our God and set a guard as a protection against them day and night (Nehemiah 4:8-9).

1. Establish a consistent, preferably weekly, time of prayer with a core group of believers with a heart for the city.

And let us consider how to stir up one another to love and good works, not neglecting to meet together, as is the habit of some, but encouraging one another, and all the more as you see the Day drawing near (Hebrews 10:24-25).

It's not the size of the group that matters as much as a firm commitment to consistently and faithfully pray for the city.

To be a true "community" prayer group with corporate authority in prayer, seek participation with believers and spiritual leaders from across the city and not just one fellowship.

2. Build your unity around the person of Jesus Christ, the truth of His Word, and the power and leading of the Holy Spirit.

Make every effort to keep the unity of the Spirit through the bond of peace. There is one body and one Spirit, just as you were called to one hope when you were called; one Lord, one faith, one baptism; one God and Father of all, who is over all and through all and in all (Ephesians 4:3-6 NIV).

As believers, our unity must be based on the Person of Jesus Christ, not a doctrine, ideology, or ministry agenda.

Choose your battles. Don't get distracted by side issues—keep your focus on becoming a community where God's tangible peace and presence can dwell.

3. Focus on what God is doing more than what the enemy is doing.

Come and see what God has done: he is awesome in his deeds toward the children of man (Psalm 66:5).

Look for indicators of God's blessing and favor, and bless what He is already doing in the city. Come into agreement with what God has spoken through His Word.

Keep praise central. The high praises of God's people has power to bring down strongholds. *"And when they began to sing and praise, the Lord set an ambush against the men of Ammon, Moab, and*

Mount Seir, who had come against Judah, so that they were routed" (2 Chronicles 20:22)

4. As issues arise, deal with them through repentance and forgiveness.

> *Then he said to me, "Fear not, Daniel, for from the first day that you set your heart to understand and humbled yourself before your God, your words have been heard, and I have come because of your words" (Daniel 10:12).*

Unresolved sin issues become open doors for the enemy. As the Holy Spirit reveals root issues on the land, ask the Lord for wisdom and take steps to clear the land of any sin, immorality, bloodshed, broken covenants, or idolatry through prayers of repentance, both personally and corporately.

When appropriate, go on-site to the places where the Lord has revealed any defilement and take communion, pray, and worship in order to cleanse the land.

5. Maintain a heart of humility and walk in the Fear of the Lord.

> *Behold, the eye of the Lord is on those who fear him, on those who hope in his steadfast love (Psalm 33:18).*

Honor those in spiritual authority; bless them and pray for them, even those you disagree with (see 1 Timothy 2:2).

Determine to walk "offense free" and practice forgiveness and forbearance toward others.

6. Build trusted relationships with other catalytic leaders.

And though a man might prevail against one who is alone, two will withstand him—a threefold cord is not quickly broken (Ecclesiastes 4:12).

These leaders may not be in the church, but in business, education, entertainment, government, and other sectors of your city. Strive to work together toward Kingdom-centered values and presence-based community transformation.

Seek to establish an atmosphere in the city where all believers are inspired to be bold witnesses for Christ.

7. Establish prayer altars throughout the city.

And David built there an altar to the Lord and offered burnt offerings and peace offerings. So the Lord responded to the plea for the land, and the plague was averted from Israel (2 Samuel 24:25).

Prayer altars help to establish a wall of prayer around a city. *"I am with you, and no one will attack you to harm you, for I have many in this city who are my people"* (Acts 18:10).

Whether they are in schools, workplaces, offices, city streets, or churches, intercessory groups become living altars where the incense of their prayers and worship ascend to heaven on behalf of the city. *"Fire shall be kept burning on the altar continually; it shall not go out"* (Leviticus 6:13).

8. Look for opportunities to be a corporate witness to the power of Christ.

May the God of endurance and encouragement grant you to live in such harmony with one another, in accord with Christ Jesus, that together you may with one voice glorify the God and Father of our Lord Jesus Christ (Romans 15:5-6).

When appropriate, demonstrate the oneness of Christ in the public square. A corporate witness and testimony have authority in the spirit to thwart any scheme of the enemy.

Pray for spiritual leaders to speak with one voice in the city and give godly wisdom when faced with threats of danger.

9. Speak well of your city and bless it with your words and your works.

They shall build up the ancient ruins; they shall raise up the former devastations; they shall repair the ruined cities, the devastations of many generations (Isaiah 61:4).

Speaking blessings on a city releases favor, especially to those who lead it. Determine to nullify any curses spoken by speaking the opposite, declaring God's Word and promises.

Put your prayers into action and look for ways to demonstrate the kindness of God through acts of compassion.

Violence shall no more be heard in your land, devastation or destruction within your borders; you shall call your walls Salvation, and your gates Praise (Isaiah 60:18).

Chapter 12

The CALL
to DISCIPLE
NATIONS

A Legacy to Fight For

Contending for Our Legacy

What we are aiming for in this journey is not simply a strong government, a healthy church, or a stable community. Our collective mandate is to establish the Kingdom of heaven here on the earth for generations to come. Our heavenly Father wants us to rule and reign with Him and it requires learning how to rule in the midst of our enemies.

However, the outcome of this journey and our corporate success in fulfilling our mandate will only be as strong as our relationships with one another. The new wineskins the Lord is forming in this Kingdom age are built on relationships, not structures. Any organization or infrastructure is only as good as the relationships of those within them.

Ultimately, Kingdom relationships are built and nurtured within the context of family. It is the fathers and mothers, the sons and daughters, and the ways we live and interact with one another that will outlive any structures we create. With the constantly changing times and seasons, this is the joy and the challenge in constantly adjusting our means and methods, while keeping our relationships intact and growing.

As I have shared in the previous chapters, how we relate to one another and work together will determine the speed, the quality, and the depth of our impact on the culture around us. Each individual will be tested in this ability to get along with others in learning how to fulfill their call while serving others. For me, this has been the story of my life—learning what family is, and isn't. We won't always agree on everything, but we need to agree on the most important things. I know this from my own upbringing in a family that probably looks a little like the Body of Christ.

My paternal grandmother was Irish Catholic. My maternal grandparents were Amish. My father was a first generation Christian and my mother was Mennonite. My father became an evangelist who reached out to the homeless and spoke in many denominations through his years. As a youth I attended a neighborhood Evangelical Free Church. My next-door neighbor was a Catholic and my best friend in high school was Methodist. I married a Spirit-filled Mennonite and we went to a Charismatic university—Oral Roberts—where we also interned at a Methodist church. My oldest brother was a cessationist. My oldest sister married a Baptist, and my other sister married a Lutheran. My younger brother loves Jesus but doesn't go to church anywhere.

Can you imagine what our family reunions are like?!

I've learned how to keep first things first because we're family. Family—just like the Body of Christ—is, first and foremost, about relationships. Regardless of our denominational preferences, doctrinal views, and even personal experiences, our unity should come from our love for Christ and the core dogmas of our faith. We can confront each other in love, agree to disagree, and stay the course in difficult times. I've never compromised my beliefs by loving my family and haven't been afraid to challenge them. The reality is that my siblings and I will probably never attend the same church. But that's okay. In the end, it's not about me, or them. It's about *us*— because we're family.

I believe this same kind of perspective and attitude can permeate the Body of Christ as we learn to partner together for a Kingdom cause. It's this God-given love for others that must be sustained as we learn how to reign in the midst of darkness. It is only by the Spirit and from the place of prayer that we will receive the kind of passion for His Bride to keep us together in hard times. When we have a unified vision for where are we headed and why, we will have a legacy worth fighting for.

The Faith of Abraham and Birthing of Nations

That is why it depends on faith, in order that the promise may rest on grace and be guaranteed to all his offspring—not only to the adherent of the law but also to the one who shares the faith of Abraham, who is the father of us all, as it is written, "I have made you the father of many nations..." (Romans 4:16-17).

Abraham is known as the father of our faith. Through his life of obedience and determination to trust God, he became the father of Israel and the standard for all who are called to father and mother nations. Giving birth to a nation may seem to be a tall order, and yet this is the kind of long-term vision that must be embraced and stewarded if we are to see righteous rule for generations to come. We need to get beyond our current problem mentality and begin to see the promise of our future.

Regardless of one's eschatology, God's plan for His creation remains, and that is to rule and reign with Him in His ever-increasing government. Rather than trying to figure out how this is going to happen, we simply need to do our part in stewarding what He has already given us and prepare our sons and daughters for their role in the journey.

One of the biggest factors in Abraham's journey that is missed in our day and age is the power of intergenerational relationships. In Abraham's day, people lived a lot longer. Parents lived long enough to see not only their grandchildren grow up, but in some cases, up to ten generations succeed them while they were still alive!

Methuselah lived the longest at 969 (see Genesis 5:27). Many other patriarchs lived for hundreds of years, enabling them to share their stories and pass on their legacy for many generations (see Genesis 5:4-31). Noah lived for 350 years after the flood and the book of Jasher, an apocryphal book mentioned twice in Scripture, suggests Abraham lived with Noah and his son Shem for 39 years (Jasher 9:4-6).

> *Abram was in Noah's house thirty-nine years, and Abram knew Yehovah from three years old, and he went in the ways of Yehovah until the day of his death, as Noah and his son Shem had taught him* (Jasher 9:6).

Though Jasher is not considered holy writ, the biblical genealogical timeline indicates this kind of relationship could have happened. If so, remember that Noah knew Methuselah, who knew Adam. This would have given Abraham access to reliable information about everything that happened since the first day of creation! Consider the power of young Abraham spending close to forty years being discipled by a father and son who had lived before, during, and after the flood, for centuries! No wonder his faith would have been so strong.

Abraham also demonstrated a three-generation principle in birthing a nation and seeing a promise fulfilled. God even told Moses He was the *God of Abraham, Isaac, and Jacob* (see Exodus 3:6). The strategy for birthing a nation through an intergenerational partnership was divinely orchestrated by God. Abraham was chosen as the father of a nation, not because of his great faith, but because God knew he would be faithful to teach his children, and all those after him, the ways of God.

The Lord said, "Shall I hide from Abraham what I am about to do, seeing that Abraham shall surely become a great and mighty nation, and all the nations of the earth shall be blessed in him? For I have chosen him, that he may command his children and his household after him to keep the way of the Lord by doing righteousness and justice, so that the Lord may bring to Abraham what he has promised him" (Genesis 18:17-19).

This three-generation partnership is something that is plausible today and one that needs attention. In our generation, we have lost the power of storytelling and oral tradition and traded it in for soundbites on social media. We have forgotten how to share our history and recite the powerful lessons of the past. Even as we pursue new wineskins and fresh expressions of the Kingdom, there are timeless truths and foundational realities that cannot be lost.

Fathers and mothers need to start writing down their stories and recording them for future generations.

And now, go, write it before them on a tablet and inscribe it in a book, that it may be for the time to come as a witness forever (Isaiah 30:8).

We must look for God-appointed opportunities to share these stories with our sons and daughters in a life-giving way that stirs and motivates them for their own future. It will also require the sons and daughters to celebrate the previous generation for the victories won and lessons learned. Rather than assuming our journeys are outdated and irrelevant, new generations need a revelation of how their lineage can impact their future. It's when we realize we truly need one another to make this work, things can begin to change.

Patriarchs and Matriarchs and Discipling Nations

Thankfully, heaven has been preparing the way. There is a rising group of men and women of God who have been hidden but have been prepared for this very mission. They are being called by the Spirit of God to prepare a future generation of Kingdom ambassadors who are going to shift culture and transform the earth. They are waking up to the reality that their journey has not been about them, but those *following them.*

The Lord is calling forth these history-makers who carry a burden for family and a vision for Kingdom expansion. Rather than seeking their own platform, they are creating platforms for their sons and daughters. The Lord is raising up these men and women of God who have the *faith of Abraham* to contend for a future generation. These are men and women with a God-given passion, zeal, and prophetic burden for their posterity—their sons and daughters after them. These are present-day "saints of old" whom heaven is drawing, empowering, and granting increased favor to in order to establish a legacy so secure and a generation so powerful, nothing will stop the increase of His government on the earth.

> *Now faith is the assurance of things hoped for, the conviction of things not seen. For by it the people of old received their commendation* (Hebrews 11:1-2).

The prophesied sons and daughters who are now emerging in this generation (see Romans 8:19) cannot mature and develop apart from spiritual fathers and mothers who nurture and disciple them. Beyond academic training and ministry development, it is the heart of fathers and mothers to build character from the inside out. They are the ones who walk alongside these future change agents through the various seasons of life to impart the grace, perspective, and needed wisdom to withstand the coming storms. **Heaven is calling forth these patriarchs and matriarchs with a vision beyond themselves to disciple entire nations** (see Genesis 17:5). Hebrews Hall of Fame for history-makers is calling forth new candidates with this same vision for heaven's promise.

> *And all these, though commended through their faith, did not receive what was promised, since God had provided something better for us, that apart from us they should not be made perfect* (Hebrews 11:39-40).

I once had a dream where I gave birth to a baby and within a few hours, I was cradling this small child in my arms on top of a platform where I presented the child to the world. The growth and development of this gifted child happened very quickly, and it was obviously supernatural. It was a dramatic illustration that the most powerful platforms needed for the emerging sons and daughters will be established through fathers and mothers. These platforms will help build and establish a lineage of rulers and agents of transformation.

In order to secure our inheritance as a royal priesthood and a holy nation (see 1 Peter 2:9), the Lord is placing within many fathers and mothers an unshakeable conviction of what is yet to come—a manifestation of heaven on earth released through their sons and daughters.

> *And he will go before him in the spirit and power of Elijah, to turn the hearts of the fathers to the children, and the disobedient to the wisdom of the just, to make ready for the Lord a people prepared* (Luke 1:17).

I also believe that many fathers and mothers who are answering this call are being endowed with long lives and vibrant health so that they can journey with the generations that follow them. This is one reason why many in the Body of Christ have taken greater interest in their personal health, many revising their diets and nutrition in order to be more productive in the years ahead. Heaven has prepared us for this hour as the rising Ekklesia of God is taking ownership in and responsibility for the legacy that follows us.

> *You shall walk in all the way that the Lord your God has commanded you, that you may live, and that it may go well with you, and that you may live long in the land that you shall possess* (Deuteronomy 5:33).

> *Honor your father and mother (this is the first commandment with a promise), that it may go well with you and that you may live long in the land* (Ephesians 6:2-3).

As much as we need to embrace five-fold equippers in this season of empowering the Body of Christ, these gifts to the Church have an expiration date. They have been given for a season. Whether or not we will be known in heaven as a prophet or an apostle will mean little if we did not disciple our young. Because the Kingdom is a family unit, I am praying that we will begin to esteem our roles as members of God's household as even more powerful and critical than our spiritual gifts. It is when we see our future as an eternal family that we will have the proper motivation to fulfill our call to rule here on the earth as it is in heaven.

PRAYER GUIDE

BUILDING
a LEGACY

1. **Pray for a revelation of God's plans for our descendants. Declare that they will build upon a solid foundation and advance the Kingdom in increasing measure.**

> *I will surely bless you, and I will surely multiply your offspring as the stars of heaven and as the sand that is on the seashore. And your offspring shall possess the gate of his enemies, and in your offspring shall all the nations of the earth be blessed, because you have obeyed my voice* (Genesis 22:17-18).

> *Let this be recorded for a generation to come, so that a people yet to be created may praise the Lord* (Psalm 102:18).

> *They are to do good, to be rich in good works, to be generous and ready to share, thus storing up treasure for themselves as a good foundation for the future, so that they may take hold of that which is truly life* (1 Timothy 6:18-19).

2. Pray for fathers and mothers to remain faithful and true to the Lord. Pray that the lessons of the past would be passed on with a zeal for our collective destiny to be fulfilled.

> *...which he commanded our fathers to teach to their children, that the next generation might know them, the children yet unborn, and arise and tell them to their children, so that they should set their hope in God and not forget the works of God, but keep his commandments* (Psalm 78:5-7).

> *I will multiply your offspring as the stars of heaven and will give to your offspring all these lands. And in your offspring all the nations of the earth shall be blessed, because Abraham obeyed my voice and kept my charge, my commandments, my statutes, and my laws* (Genesis 26:4-5).

> *For I have chosen him, that he may command his children and his household after him to keep the way of the Lord by doing righteousness and justice, so that the Lord may bring to Abraham what He has promised him* (Genesis 18:19).

3. Pray that the younger generation would honor and esteem the elders and forefathers for their battles fought and victories won. Pray for open hearts and inquisitive minds to hear the stories of God's faithfulness.

> *Remember the days of old; consider the years of many generations; ask your father, and he will show you, your elders, and they will tell you* (Deuteronomy 32:7).

> *For inquire, please, of bygone ages, and consider what the fathers have searched out. For we are but of yesterday and*

know nothing, for our days on earth are a shadow. Will they not teach you and tell you and utter words out of their understanding? (Job 8:8-10)

4. Declare that, through our collective vision, the Kingdom of God will continue to increase and advance.

Your kingdom is an everlasting kingdom, and your dominion endures throughout all generations... (Psalm 145:13).

...that they may be called oaks of righteousness, the planting of the Lord, that he may be glorified. They shall build up the ancient ruins; they shall raise up the former devastations; they shall repair the ruined cities, the devastations of many generations (Isaiah 61:3-4).

ABOUT *the* AUTHOR

Wanda Alger is a recognized five-fold prophetic minister and a writer with Intercessors for America. She has authored numerous books and her articles have been published with *Christian Post, Charisma, The Elijah List,* and *Spirit Fuel.* She ministers with her husband, Pastor Bobby Alger, in Winchester, Virginia, at Crossroads Community Church that they planted in 1998. They have three grown children.

ALSO *by* WANDA ALGER *from* DESTINY IMAGE

Prayer That Sparks National Revival:
An Essential Guide for Reclaiming America's Destiny

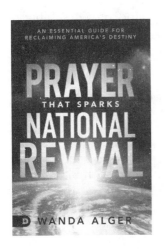

The kind of prayer that sparks and shifts a nation must go beyond personal desire to corporate agreement. We need to find common ground in the midst of extremist views and divisive rhetoric so we can rise with one voice and one message as the Ekklesia of God.

This prayer manual includes several strategic prayer outlines that can be used for effective corporate intercession, in addition to a prophetic perspective on our national crisis and the current mandate of the Church.

Additional Resources from wandaalger.me

Oracles of Grace:
Building a Legacy of Wisdom and Revelation

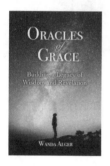

A new devotional resource to take you deeper in your walk with the Lord. Over 40 entries of prophetic insights and scriptural principles to build a lasting foundation in your journey as a Spirit-empowered believer.

Making Room for His Presence:
A 21-Day Community Fast Devotional Guide

This 21-day prayer guide provides biblical admonitions and practical prayer points that will help prepare the way for a deeper experience of God's presence in your own life. When prayed in a community, it can open the door to a greater experience of God's presence in your church and community.

- *Pastors, Prophets, and Intercessors DVD Teachings* with Bill Yount, Brian Francis Hume, and Bobby Alger

- *Dream Interpretation CD Series*

- *Prophetic Coaching Seminar DVD*

Follow Wanda's Blog at www.wandaalger.me

Join to receive weekly email posts:

- Prophetic perspectives on current issues

- Teaching articles

- Prayer resources

- Video clips

- DVD and CD Teaching Resources

Provide your email and automatically receive new postings to your inbox, receiving fresh devotional thoughts to stir your spirit and grow your faith.

PRAYER RESOURCES from
INTERCESSORS FOR AMERICA

IFAPRAY.ORG

Headline Prayer: News Christians need to pray about *EVERY DAY*

FRANKLIN GRAHAM CALLS FOR DAY OF PRAYER FOR PRES. TRUMP SUNDAY, JUNE 2
MAY 31, 2019

Heavenly Father, let there be a loud cry of support for our President this Sunday...

Evangelist, Franklin Graham is calling Christians across the nation to join him and other leaders in a day of prayer for President Trump this Sunday, June 2. In his Facebook...

LOUISIANA DEMOCRATIC GOVERNOR SIGNS HEARTBEAT BILL
MAY 31, 2019

Thank you Lord, for this governor, who is standing firm for life, even against his...

As Louisiana joins the ranks of states passing heartbeat abortion bans, the case is highlighting a growing effort by Democrat leaders to reject all pro-lifers from their party. Louisiana's Democratic...

WHY ARE SOME PRO-LIFE MINISTRIES AND LEADERS FIGHTING TO KEEP ABORTION?
MAY 31, 2019

Lord, forgive us for our inability to grasp that simply restricting abortion still accepts it....

The fight challenging the legality of abortion has never been more intense. Every month new laws are brought to a vote across our land as state after state reveals their...

HEADLINE PRAYER: News Christians Need to Read About Every Day – Scroll through this daily feed of national headlines, devotionals, articles, prophetic words, and other resources to fuel your daily prayer with prophetic insight and targeted intercession.

INTERACTIVE NATIONAL PRAYER MAP – Find intercessors and prayer groups near you with a similar passion in praying for your community and nation.

INTERACTIVE PRAYER WALL – A 24/7 wall of prayer for the nation where intercessors can interact in real time for one-hour increments.

THE INFORMER

CRITICAL ISSUES WITH WEIGHTY CONSEQUENCES NEED YOUR PRAYER

'WHATEVER IT TAKES': AS GOVERNMENT STARTS TO REOPEN

Please pray that our governmental policies will be held to the highest standards of good governance. [B]...

READ MORE & PRAY

VERMONT'S RADICAL BILL TO PROTECT 'FUNDAMENTAL RIGHT' TO ...

Pray that this bill will be blocked and that the death of future generations will be thwarted. ...

READ MORE & PRAY

TERRORIST AT HEAD OF DRUG CARTEL ON TEXAS BORDER

Pray for our law enforcement officers along our southern border. Pray for wisdom and their protection as ...

READ MORE & PRAY

MASS NON-CITIZEN VOTING IN TEXAS EXPOSED

Pray for a restoration legal voting throughout our nation and that corrupt organizations will be found and ...

Have you prayed for Donald Trump?
President

I PRAYED

THE INFORMER – Join this free email list to receive three weekly email alerts with urgent prayer needs, timely articles, and devotional helps for informed intercession.

IFA FACEBOOK – Join the growing community of intercessors online.

Access free Prayer Guides, Special Reports, and Devotionals to use for personal intercession and small group prayer.

Experience a personal revival!

Spirit-empowered content from today's top Christian authors delivered directly to your inbox.

Join today!
lovetoreadclub.com

Inspiring Articles
Powerful Video Teaching
Resources for Revival

Get all of this and so much more, e-mailed to you twice weekly!

LOVE TO READ CLUB

by 𝔇 DESTINY IMAGE